Romeo & Juliet

ADVISORY EDITORS

DAVID BEVINGTON, BARBARA GAINES, AND PETER HOLLAND

SERIES EDITORS

MARIE MACAISA AND DOMINIQUE RACCAH

William Shakspeare

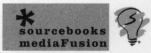

sourcebooks mediaFusion

An Imprint of Sourcebooks Inc.®
Naperville, Illinois

Audio and photo credits are found at the end of the book.

Published by Sourcebooks, Inc.
P.O. Box 4410, Naperville, Illinois   60567-4410
(630) 961-3900
Fax: (630) 961-2168
www.sourcebooks.com

Library of Congress Cataloging-in-Publication Data

Shakespeare, William, 1564-1616.
  Romeo and Juliet / William Shakespeare ; Marie Macaisa, editor.
     p. cm.
  Includes index.
  ISBN 1-4022-0644-5 (alk. paper) -- ISBN 1-4022-0101-X (pbk. : alk. paper) 1. Romeo (Fictitious character)--Drama. 2. Juliet (Fictitious character)--Drama. 3. Conflict of generations--Drama. 4. Verona (Italy)--Drama. 5. Vendetta--Drama. I. Macaisa, Marie. II. Title.

PR2831.A2M26 2005
822.3'3--dc22

                                  2005023286

Printed and bound in the United States of America.
LB   10   9   8   7   6   5   4   3   2   1

To students, teachers, and lovers of Shakespeare

Contents

On the CD

The audio selections bring Shakespeare's words to life, showing you different ways in which speeches have been interpreted by some of the greatest Shakespeareans of all time.

1. Nurse, where's my daughter? 1.3.1–1.3.68
   Fiona Shaw as the Nurse, Frances Barber as Lady Capulet
2. Nurse, where's my daughter? 1.3.1–1.3.68
   Dame Flora Robson as the Nurse, Virginia McKenna as Juliet, Rachel Kempson as Lady Capulet
3. O, then I see Queen Mab hath been with you 1.4.57–1.4.109
   Anton Lesser as Mercutio, Michael Sheen as Romeo
4. O, then I see Queen Mab hath been with you 1.4.57–1.4.101
   Ian Bannen as Mercutio, Keith Michell as Romeo
5. If I profane with my unworthiest hand 1.5.95–1.5.112
   Estelle Kohler as Juliet, Bill Homewood as Romeo
6. If I profane with my unworthiest hand 1.5.95–1.5.112
   Kate Beckinsale as Juliet, Michael Sheen as Romeo
7. But soft, what light through yonder window breaks? 2.2.2–2.2.34
   Joseph Fiennes as Romeo, Maria Miles as Juliet
8. But soft, what light through yonder window breaks? 2.2.2–2.2.34
   Albert Finney as Romeo, Claire Bloom as Juliet
9. Romeo, Romeo–wherefore art thou, Romeo 2.2.35–2.2.85
   Joseph Fiennes as Romeo, Maria Miles as Juliet
10. Romeo, Romeo–wherefore art thou, Romeo 2.2.35–2.2.85
    Albert Finney as Romeo, Claire Bloom as Juliet
11. Tybalt, you ratcatcher 3.1.65–3.1.127
    Anton Lesser as Mercutio, Jasper Britton as Tybalt, Michael Sheen as Romeo, Claire Bloom as Juliet
12. Tybalt, you ratcatcher 3.1.65–3.1.127
    Ian Bannen as Mercutio, Nigel Davenport as Tybalt, Keith Michell as Romeo
13. There's no trust 3.2.88–3.2.130
    Dame Judi Dench as the Nurse, Samantha Bond as Juliet

14. There is no world without Verona walls 3.3.18–3.3.77
    Kenneth Branagh as Romeo, Sir John Gielgud as Friar Laurence
15. Hold thy desperate hand! 3.3.108–3.3.165
    Sir John Gielgud as Friar Laurence, Kenneth Branagh as Romeo,
    Dame Judi Dench as the Nurse
16. Wilt thou be gone? Is it not yet near day 3.5.1–3.5.36
    Kate Beckinsale as Juliet, Michael Sheen as Romeo
17. Wilt thou be gone? Is it not yet near day 3.5.1–3.5.36
    Claire Bloom as Juliet, Albert Finney as Romeo
18. Farewell! God knows when we shall meet again 4.3.15–4.3.59
    Dame Peggy Ashcroft as Juliet
19. Farewell! God knows when we shall meet again 4.3.15–4.3.59
    Virginia McKenna as Juliet
20. (BONUS) Farewell! God knows when we shall meet again 4.3.15–4.3.59
    Ellen Terry as Juliet
21. Speaking Shakespeare, Act 1 Prologue
    Andrew Wade with members of the Guthrie Experience for Actors in
    Training

Note from the Series Editors

For many of us, our first and only encounter with Shakespeare was in school. We may recall that experience as a struggle, working through dense texts, filled with unfamiliar words. However, those of us who were fortunate enough to have seen a play performed may have altogether different memories. It may be of an interesting scene or an unusual character, but it is most likely a speech. Often, just hearing part of one instantly transports us to that time and place. "Friends, Romans, countrymen, lend me your ears," "But, soft! What light through yonder window breaks?," "To sleep, perchance to dream," "Tomorrow, and tomorrow, and tomorrow."

The Sourcebooks Shakespeare series is our attempt to use the power of performance to help you experience the play. In it, you will see photographs from various productions, on film and on stage, historical and contemporary, known worldwide or in your community. You may even learn of some popular actors' surprising Shakespearean performances. You will see set drawings, costume designs, and scene edits, all reproduced from original notes. Finally, on the enclosed audio CD, you will hear scenes from the play as performed by some of the most accomplished Shakespeareans of our times. Often, we include multiple interpretations of the same scene, showing you the remarkable richness of the text. Hear the great Ellen Terry in a 1911 recording the scene where Juliet prepares to take the potion prepared for her by the Friar. Compare that to Kate Beckinsale in a modern version made in 1997. The actors are using the same words but they make the speech create different Juliets.

As you read the text of the play, you can consult explanatory notes for definitions of unfamiliar words and phrases or words whose meanings have changed. These notes appear on the left pages, next to the text of the play. The audio, photographs, and other production artifacts augment the notes, and they too are indexed to the appropriate lines. You can use the pictures to see how others have staged a particular scene and get ideas on costumes, scenery, and blocking. As for the audio, each track represents a particular interpretation of a scene. Sometimes, a passage that's difficult to comprehend opens up when you hear it out loud. Furthermore, when you hear more than one version, you gain a keener understanding of the characters. Was Emilia a victim of domestic violence? Was Mercutio in love with Romeo? Was Hamlet depressed or suicidal? The actors made their choices and so can you. You may even come up with your own interpretation.

The text of the play, the definitions, the production notes, the audio—all of these go together, and they are here for your enjoyment. The audio, being excerpts of performances, is meant to entertain. When you see a passage with an associated clip, you can read along as you hear the actors perform the scenes for you. Or, you can sit back, close your eyes, and listen, and then go back and reread the text with a new perspective. Finally, since the text is actually a script, you may find yourself reciting the lines out loud and doing your own performance!

You will undoubtedly notice that some of the audio does not exactly match the text. Also, there are photographs and facsimiles of scenes that aren't in your edition. There are many reasons for this, but foremost among them is the fact that Shakespeare scholarship continues to move forward and the prescribed ways of dealing with and interpreting text is always changing. Thus a play that was edited and published in 1944 will be different from one published in 2005. It may also surprise you to know that there frequently isn't one definitive early edition of each play. *Romeo and Juliet*, for example, appeared in seven editions before 1642. The first quarto, published in 1597, was based on a reconstruction from memory by a group familiar with the production. The second quarto, described on the cover as "newly corrected, augmented, and amended," is 50 percent longer than the first. Finally, artists have their own interpretation of the play and they too cut and change lines and scenes according to their vision. Garrick famously added a funeral scene for Juliet; Kemble cut all mention of Romeo's first love interest, Rosaline. And, according to Professor Jill L. Levenson, "When Zeffirelli and his screenwriters had finished with Shakespeare's lines, only a third of them remained, and that third differs noticeably from the original."

There's been barely a year since its first appearance that *Romeo and Juliet* hasn't been performed somewhere in the world. However, the way in which it has been presented has varied considerably through the years. We've included essays in the book to give you glimpses into the range of the productions, show-ing you how other artists have approached the play and providing examples of just what changes were made and how. David Bevington's essay on the 1811 production as it was performed in Covent Garden in London shows you how the play was typically staged in the early 1800s. Jill L. Levenson discusses the performance history of the play in her essay, "In Production," covering key historical versions such as Garrick's and Cushman's and more modern ones from Gielgud, Brook, and Zeffirelli. Douglas Lanier's essay, "What's in a Name?," presents an intriguing look at how the play has been appropriated, twisted, and adapted by popular culture. He cites at least seven examples of Romeo-and-Juliet pairs, ill-fated lovers who come from vastly different, some-times opposite cultures, including: African Americans and immigrants from India, law enforcers and pornographers, valley girls and city punkers, and mutants and normals. Finally, for the actor in you (or for those of you who want to look behind the curtain), we have two essays that you may find intriguing. Andrew Wade, voice coach of the Royal Shakespeare Company for thirteen years, shares his point of view on how to understand the text and speak it. You will also hear him working with actors on the audio CD so that you too can learn the art of speaking Shakespeare. The last essay, "The Cast Speaks," is actually from an interview we conducted. We talked to each member of a cast (in this case, Chicago Shakespeare Theater in their 2005 pro-duction) about their characters and relationships. It is fascinating to hear the performers' own takes on their characters: the friendship between Romeo and Mercutio, Juliet's perplexing personality, the Capulets' intentions, the hidden opinions of the Nurse and the Friar. The characters come to life in a way that's different from just reading the play or even watching a performance.

One last note: we are frequently asked why we didn't include the whole play, either in audio or video. While we enjoy the plays and are avid theatergoers, we are trying to do something more with the audio (and the production notes and essays) than just presenting them to you. In fact, our goal is to provide you tools that will enable you to explore the play on your own, from many different directions. Our hope is that the different pieces of audio, the voices of the actors, old production photos and notes, all these will engage you and illuminate the play in various ways so that you can construct your own understanding and create your own production, as it were.

Though the productions we referenced and the audio clips we have included are but a miniscule sample of the play's history, we hope they encourage you to further delve into the works of Shakespeare. New editions of the play come out yearly, movie adaptations are regularly being produced, there are hundreds of theater groups in the U.S. alone, and performances could be going on right in your backyard. We echo the words of noted writer and poet Robert Graves, who said, "The remarkable thing about Shakespeare is that he is really very good—in spite of all the people who say he is very good."

We welcome you now to The Sourcebooks Shakespeare edition of *Romeo and Juliet*.

Dominique Raccah and Marie Macaisa
Series Editors

In Production:

ROMEO & JULIET THROUGH THE YEARS

Jill L. Levenson

Shakespeare's *Romeo and Juliet* has had an incredible career on the stage since its first performances at the end of the sixteenth century. From the Restoration on it has been in production—in one form or another—almost continuously. During certain periods it has enjoyed enormous success. The second half of the eighteenth century was one of those times: there were 399 performances in London between 1751 and 1800, eclipsing *Hamlet*. The second half of the twentieth century, through the millennium, has seen hundreds of revivals internationally, and only *Hamlet* has eclipsed *Romeo and Juliet*.

It is probably the story of Romeo and Juliet which attracts audiences of different backgrounds and all ages: the narrative derives from a myth about youthful passion that accepts no limits, about lovers who die in their attempt to cross impossible boundaries. The myth is also about rites of passage, transitions in an individual life from one biological or social condition to another. In the famous love stories where it appears, it centers the narrative on young love: the myth and its literary versions catch the lovers at the moment of change, failing to make the transition into the community. As part of this tradition, Shakespeare's play catches them specifically in the early and middle phases of adolescence. Its portrayal of these phases is remarkable for its accuracy and thoroughness, and it may explain the play's timeless appeal to teenagers and to adults still in touch with their earlier selves.

In its composition *Romeo and Juliet* executes a tour de force, a brilliant play on the dramatic and literary conventions of its age: it rewrites the novella or short-fiction version of the love story as a tragic drama incorporating comedy and forms of Renaissance verse. Whatever its sources, however, the circumstances of its first productions must have vitalized every aspect of its creation. Shakespeare may have written the tragedy during a period of theatrical disorganization in England, but the uncertainties caused by the plague and politics—the closing of the London theaters in 1592–1593 and the rearrangement of established companies—had passed before the first performances. Consequently, *Romeo and Juliet* premiered in the extraordinary theatrical scene taking shape during the last years of the sixteenth century: a particular company, sharing a particular style of performance, enacted the play for audiences in Elizabethan public theaters. Actors from Shakespeare's company, the Chamberlain's Men, vocalized the written words as prosody, stage directions, content, and perhaps Shakespeare himself directed. They brought the play to life in the mid-to-late 1590s on an open stage, probably first at the Theatre and then at the Curtain.

The stylization of *Romeo and Juliet*—its use of verse and other formal conventions to retell the familiar love story—has posed a serious challenge to performers in the eras which followed its introduction to the stage. As a result, productions since the late seventeenth century have made significant adjustments to Shakespeare's text. Not surprisingly, these adjustments always reflect the theatrical conventions of the period, and sometimes they reflect political circumstances as well. For instance, the first version of *Romeo and Juliet* that survived from the Restoration adapts about 750 lines

THE
HISTORY and FALL
OF
Caius Marius.
A
TRAGEDY.
As it is Acted at the
Duke's Theatre.

By *Thomas Otway.*

Qui color Albus erat nunc est contrarius Albo.

LONDON,
Printed for *Tho. Flesher,* at the *Angel and Crown*
in S. *Paul's Church-yard,* 1680.

Persons represented.

Men	By
Caius Marius.	Mr. *Betterton.*
Sylla.	Mr. *Williams.*
Marius junior.	Mr. *Smith.*
Granius.	Mr. *Percivale.*
Metellus.	Mr. *Gillow.*
Quintus Pompeius.	Mr. *Williams.*
Cinna.	Mr. *Jevon.*
Sulpitius.	Mr. *Underhill.*
Ancharius a Senatour.	
Priest.	
Apothecary.	
Q. Pompeius's Son.	
Guards, Lictors,	
Ruffians, &c.	

Women	By
Lavinia.	Mrs. *Barry.*
Nurse.	Mr. *Noakes.*

THE

Playbill for Otway's adaptation

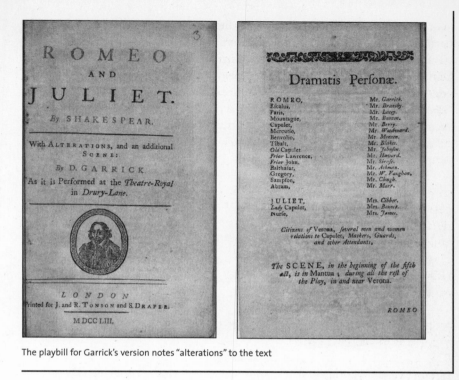

The playbill for Garrick's version notes "alterations" to the text

from Shakespeare's play (about 25 percent) to a story about conflict in republican Rome. Called *The History and Fall of Caius Marius*, it turns the feud into a civil war to warn its audience about the evils of such conflict. The author of the adaptation, Thomas Otway, was writing in 1679, a time of great political instability in England. In his play the lovers represent virtue overwhelmed by civil chaos.

Otway's tragedy may be unknown now, but it displaced Shakespeare's play for fifty-five years, and it inaugurated the long-run versions of *Romeo and Juliet* which have occupied English-speaking theaters through the late twentieth century and into the beginning of the twenty-first. With *Romeo and Juliet*, theater history has had a noticeable pattern. Some theater person produces a version of the tragedy that catches on—it might be a playwright, or an actor/manager, or a director—and that version holds the stage for at least a few decades. In the history of the play until the present, there have been five of these influential productions.

The most successful version of *Romeo and Juliet* ever was probably David Garrick's, first performed in 1748; it held the stage for almost a century—a very long run. History moved on, culture changed, but Garrick's *Romeo and Juliet* continued in performance until the middle of the nineteenth century, even though it had been created to satisfy the standards and taste of the mid-eighteenth century. Garrick was an entrepreneur who bowed to his audience's

David Garrick as Romeo and George Ann Bellamy as Juliet. Based on a painting by Benjamin Wilson engraved by Ravenet, ca. 1765

wishes in making adjustments to Shakespeare's text: he shortened the tragedy, cut out its bawdiness and other puns, and turned it into the equivalent of pathetic drama, the popular form of drama in his period. In his adaptation—as in some earlier forms—Juliet wakes up in the tomb after Romeo has taken the poison and the lovers share a seventy-five-line dialogue (see pages 300-303 in the text). The trials of Garrick's protagonists bring them to the verge of madness, the ultimate in pathos. Here is Romeo, about to expire, believing that enemies are bearing down on his heart and Juliet's:

> Capulet forbear! Paris loose your hold!
> Pull not our heartstrings thus; they crack, they break.
> O! Juliet! Juliet! (*Dies*).

Garrick's *Romeo and Juliet* had one other striking aspect besides its decorum and sentimentality: Garrick made it a vehicle for two star performers, and it remained a vehicle built for two through the middle of the nineteenth century. The social and political dimensions of the tragedy virtually disappeared.

By the middle of the nineteenth century, one feature of *Romeo and Juliet* had become an embarrassment: professional male actors felt uncomfortable with the part of Romeo because it was so emotional, particularly the scene in Friar Laurence's cell where Romeo thrashes around on the floor. This may be the reason why a woman created the next very successful production. Charlotte Cushman, an American actress, revived *Romeo and Juliet* in 1845–1846, and her version was performed for more than two decades. She not only managed this production; she played the part of Romeo. Cushman's claim to fame is that she discarded Garrick's text and went back to Shakespeare, although she did make cuts which reflected the Victorian era in which she performed. Not unexpectedly, she did everything possible to

Charlotte and Susan Cushman as Romeo and Juliet

enhance the part of Romeo, and the production revolved around her portrayal. In a sense, this was the narrowest interpretation of the tragedy to date.

During the twentieth century, the turning point in stagings of *Romeo and Juliet* was John Gielgud's version in 1935: it set box-office records and influenced many later productions. Gielgud directed, and he and Laurence Olivier exchanged the roles of Romeo and Mercutio during the run. Gielgud restored the whole Shakespearean text, and he tried to perform it in a modern facsimile of Elizabethan conditions: quickly, fluently, without scene breaks, on a permanent set, and with the poetry in full flight. Although all of the play was there for the audience to appreciate, Gielgud's vision isolated the lovers of myth, the universal and transcendent lovers: Peggy Ashcroft played Juliet, and the scenes with Olivier as Romeo lit up the stage.

In the history of *Romeo and Juliet* on the stage since Shakespeare's time, this key production, central to the modern era, left few traces and remained a vague impression over the course of fifty years. For Garrick, there is a lot of published scholarship; for Cushman, there are papers at the Folger Shakespeare Library and the Library of Congress, and a printed script. But Gielgud's records had disappeared completely. There was no promptbook, that is, the script with all of the cues, technical notes, etc. This had been a commercial production at the New Theatre (now known as the Albery) shortly before World War II. The New Theatre held no records whatever of this staging; the cast had not kept their scripts; and archives like the Theatre Museum in London drew a blank on Gielgud's mounting of the play.

This situation changed unexpectedly in the mid-1980s because two people deeply invested in the history of theater unearthed and made accessible information about the Gielgud production.

First, Professor Michael A. Mullin persuaded his institution, the University of Illinois at Urbana-Champaign, to buy the entire collection of costume and stage designs by Motley, the three women who worked for Gielgud. There were slides of everything, including the 1935 *Romeo and Juliet*. Second, one of the Motley designers, Margaret "Percy" Harris, was not only alive and well (in her eighties), but still working in London, teaching stage design at the Riverside Studios. At Professor Mullin's request, she extricated from Gielgud his scrapbook of the production and she spent two days with me at the Riverside Studios going through the text of the play scene

The set design for Act 1, as staged by Sir John Gielgud in 1935
Rare Books and Special Collections Library, University of Illinois at Urbana-Champaign

by scene and with the appropriate slides. She had total recall of the cuts (there were almost none) and much of the stage business; and she did a sketch of the stage set to demonstrate how the actors moved around it. With her help, what had been a void became stage history.

The fourth and fifth major productions did not present such difficulties: they are Peter Brook's for the Royal Shakespeare Company in 1947 and Franco Zeffirelli's Old Vic stage version in 1960 (which would later be translated into his 1968 film). For Brook's staging, the Shakespeare Centre in Stratford-upon-Avon houses the promptbook, reviews, and other performance memorabilia. For Zeffirelli's two renditions, data are scattered everywhere from a theater workbook to reviews to actors' recollections.

Brook thought he was working independently, unaffected by Gielgud's innovations, and perhaps he was. While he cut many lines, Brook revived features of the tragedy which had faded, especially its social context. His production was inspired by a line at the beginning of the third act: "For now, these hot days, is the mad blood stirring"; and he claimed, "I am entirely responsible for portraying Romeo and Juliet as two children lost in the maelstrom around them...." That is, he emphasized the effects of the feud, making the public scenes fiery and violent. Brook used minimalist sets in a symbolic way that allowed the action, like Gielgud's, to move swiftly. If reviewers dismissed this original production, the public made it a box-office success; and at least one critic later reflected that this was a pivotal moment in the history of British theater, because Brook approached Shakespeare with few preconceptions and treated the text as living theater.

Olivia Hussey as Juliet and Leonard Whiting as Romeo in Zeffirelli's 1968 production
Courtesy: Douglas Lanier

As for the fifth important component of this theater history, Zeffirelli's *Romeo and Juliet* is widely known in its cinematic form, which was, by 1990, the most commercially successful Shakespeare film to date, returning over $50 million on an initial investment of $1.5 million. In both media Zeffirelli cut the text heavily—by two thousand lines in the film—used the techniques of neorealism to convey the narrative. He emphasized what the 1960s called "the generation gap," the obstructed rite of passage; and he not only appealed to the youth culture of that decade, but made his way, through videotape, into the American high school curriculum over the next twenty years or so. It remains to be seen whether Baz Luhrmann's film, which spoke so powerfully to adolescents in the late 1990s, will displace Zeffirelli's.

George Bernard Shaw believed that the stylization of Shakespeare's *Romeo and Juliet* made the characters' parts "almost impossible except to actors of positive genius." Yet five productions since the eighteenth century have shown that the play in performance can captivate a wide range of audiences. When its challenges are met—however they are met—this tragedy of young love mirrors nature with unusual intensity, no matter what the age or body of the time. Of course, adaptation is crucial, and Peter Brook describes with great insight the place of innovation in performances of even the most familiar texts:

> ... [I]f a play is revived, changes must be made ... When Garrick played *Romeo and Juliet* in knee-breeches, he was *right*; when Kean staged *The Winter's Tale* with a hundred Persian pot-carriers, he was *right*; when Tree staged Shakespeare with all the resources of His Majesty's, he was *right*; when Craig staged his reaction to this he was *right* too. Each was justified in its own time; each would be outrageous out of it. A production is only correct at the moment of its correctness, and only good at the moment of its success. In its beginning is its beginning, and in its end is its end.

David Bevington

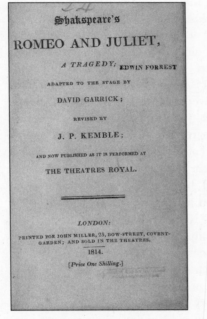

Title page from 1814 souvenir Garrick-Kemble text

Shakespeare's *Romeo and Juliet*, adapted to the stage by David Garrick and revised by John Philip Kemble, was published in a souvenir text as acted at the Theatre Royal in Covent Garden in 1810, 1811, and 1814. Garrick had been famous as Romeo starting in 1748 at the Theatre Royal in Drury Lane. Kemble, though a little old for the part, played opposite his sister, Sarah Siddons, as Juliet, in 1788 and 1789. Between them, Garrick and Kemble made *Romeo and Juliet* the most frequently performed Shakespeare play of the era. The text we have from 1811 is marked up as a promptbook by someone other than Kemble. The play it thus offers is essentially Garrick's adaptation; Kemble is a continuer of the Garrick tradition.

What we have, then, is an adapted version from the late eighteenth century. It offers us a fine glimpse into theatrical practices of that era. Though very popular still, Shakespeare's play is seen to be in need of substantial revision. Among the more striking alterations are these: Romeo is not enamored of a young lady named Rosaline at the start of the play, nor indeed is Rosaline ever mentioned. Juliet's age is advanced from "not yet fourteen" to nearly eighteen, partly perhaps so that older actresses like Sarah Siddons would not look too out-of-place in the part. Bawdry is decorously removed. Juliet appears on a balcony when she and Romeo profess their love for each other, despite the fact that Shakespeare never uses the word "balcony" in this, or any other, play; in Shakespeare's text, Juliet appears at her "window" facing out on the garden in back of her parents' house. Another distinctive change is that Juliet awakens in her tomb before Romeo actually dies, so that the lovers are given a long moment of tragic pathos. Some of these changes, including the "balcony," were inherited by Garrick and Kemble from performance traditions of the Restoration and early eighteenth century; a balcony suited well the staging methods of the era, and turns up regularly in graphic illustrations of the scene by contemporary artists.

Overall, Garrick and Kemble have redesigned the play so as to provide efficiency in the changing of sets. Whereas on Shakespeare's stage in 1594–1596 no scenery was employed and props were brought on only occasionally, Restoration and eighteenth-century staging required that each scene embody a visual representation of the required location. Flats were moved onto the stage from the wings by means of grooves in the stage floor, and the middle rearstage area was similarly provided with flats and grooves for a central display. Garrick and Kemble employed thirteen sets with which to represent twenty-six scenes, five of them identified as *The Cloisters of a Convent*, four as *A Room in Capulet's House*, and three as *Juliet's Antechamber*. In addition there are street scenes, notably the opening sequence of public brawling and then the series of clashes in which Mercutio and Tybalt are killed. *The Great Hall in Capulet's House* provides the location for the first meeting of Romeo and Juliet at the masked ball, which, because it requires

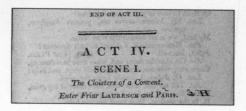

One of Garrick and Kemble's thirteen sets, *The Cloisters of a Convent*

elaborate furnishings, is to be "discovered" by the opening of curtains. Similarly, *Juliet's Chamber*, complete with bed, table, toilette, and chairs, is to be "discovered" to view for the scene in which the lovers say farewell to each other after Romeo's banishment from Verona. In Act 5, *The Monument of the Capulets* stands amidst a painted moonlit scene of a graveyard; a central opening in that monument, flanked by flats in grooves, enables the audience to see into the interior of the monument where Juliet lies.

A few instances can perhaps suffice to make clear how these economies of scene-building are achieved in the Garrick-Kemble version. The opening scene of street violence is much as in Shakespeare's text, albeit robbed of the salacious humor among the servants of the Capulet household about pushing Montague's maids to the wall and making them feel "a pretty piece of flesh." Montague, unaccompanied by his wife, learns from Benvolio about Romeo's melancholic self-imposed isolation, though with no suggestion of lovesickness over Rosaline. In Scene 2, as in Shakespeare's play, we are introduced to the rival wooer, Count Paris, whom Capulet encourages to woo Juliet at the upcoming feast. The bawdy comedy of Capulet's servant, Peter, is cut entirely. In Scene 3, Romeo confesses to Benvolio and Mercutio that he is pining away for Juliet (not Rosaline), and is urged by them to seek out new love adventures at the Capulets' masked ball. Mercutio's "Queen Mab" speech, with its wry view of love, contains no raunchy talk of maids that lie on their backs. The Nurse's rambling discourse to Juliet and Lady Capulet about weaning Juliet some fifteen years ago (the date having been adjusted to correspond with Juliet's announced age of "nearly eighteen") retains much of its Shakespearean earthiness; to be sure, "breast" is substituted for "dug" in the Nurse's account of how Juliet squirmed and recoiled "when it did taste the wormwood on the nipple of my dug," but later in the same scene the

Nurse is allowed to offer her view that Juliet has sucked wisdom from the Nurse's "teat."

The masked ball in Shakespeare's script begins in continuous action from the previous scene; Romeo, Benvolio, Mercutio and their companions, having gathered in the streets of Verona, "march about the stage" while servingmen come forth with napkins, announcing thereby that what was at first a street

Lines referring to Romeo's lovesick wanderings are crossed out.

scene has imperceptibly modulated into a brightly lit interior hall. In the absence of scenery, the Elizabethan stage can make such metamorphoses possible across nominal breaks in scenes. Not so the Garrick-Kemble version. It begins, with the aid of movable flats, as a new scene located in *A Hall in Capulet's House*. At this masked ball, Romeo recognizes Juliet across the

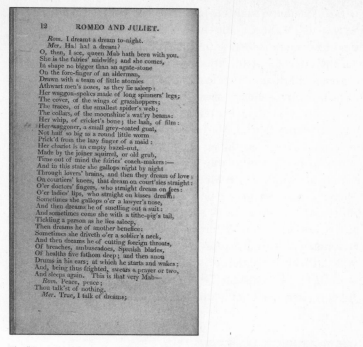

12   ROMEO AND JULIET.

Rom. I dreamt a dream to-night.
Mer. Ha! ha! a dream?
O, then, I see, queen Mab hath been with you.
She is the fairies' midwife; and she comes,
In shape no bigger than an agate-stone
On the fore-finger of an alderman,
Drawn with a team of little atomies
Athwart men's noses, as they lie asleep:
Her waggon-spokes made of long spinners' legs;
The cover, of the wings of grasshoppers;
The traces, of the smallest spider's web;
The collars, of the moonshine's wat'ry beams:
Her whip, of cricket's bone; the lash, of film:
Her waggoner, a small grey-coated gnat,
Not half so big as a round little worm
Prick'd from the lazy finger of a maid:
Her chariot is an empty hazel-nut,
Made by the joiner squirrel, or old grub,
Time out of mind the fairies' coach-makers:—
And in this state she gallops night by night
Through lovers' brains, and then they dream of love:
On courtiers' knees, that dream on court'sies straight:
O'er doctors' fingers, who straight dream on fees:
O'er ladies' lips, who straight on kisses dream:
Sometimes she gallops o'er a lawyer's nose,
And then dreams he of smelling out a suit;
And sometimes come she with a tithe-pig's tail,
Tickling a parson as he lies asleep,
Then dreams he of another benefice:
Sometimes she driveth o'er a soldier's neck,
And then dreams he of cutting foreign throats,
Of breaches, ambuscadoes, Spanish blades,
Of healths five fathom deep; and then anon
Drums in his ears; at which he starts and wakes;
And, being thus frighted, swears a prayer or two,
And sleeps again.   This is that very Mab—
Rom. Peace, peace;
Thou talk'st of nothing.
Mer. True, I talk of dreams;

The "Queen Mab" speech: the lines referring to "blisters plague," as well as the last seven lines, are cut.

crowded room, for she has long been the object of his veneration. Yet when they meet on the dance floor and exchange a few words and a kiss ("*Salutes her*," reads the Garrick-Kemble stage direction) Juliet is evidently caught by surprise, so much so that she has to ask the Nurse who it is that she has been dancing with; it is thus that Juliet learns that her new love is "Romeo, and a Montague, / The only son of your great enemy." She realizes, as in Shakespeare, that "my only love" is "sprung from my only hate." The novelty of this revelation is a little puzzling in this Garrick-Kemble version, since Romeo has worshipped Juliet for quite some time now, but this is Garrick's way of getting rid of Rosaline. Garrick is determined that Romeo be in love with Juliet from the start and with no one else.

The opening of Act 2 is indicative of a significant shift in staging methods between the late sixteenth and eighteenth centuries. Shakespeare leads off with a brief scene in which Mercutio and Benvolio come looking for Romeo as he hides from them in back of the Capulet house. On a stage with no scenery, Romeo need do nothing more elaborate than hide behind a stage pillar until they leave, at which point, without alteration of scenery, the stage is now understood to represent the orchard or garden looking up at Juliet's "window" in the theater facade backstage, in the gallery above the stage doors. For Garrick and his generation, on the other hand, an entirely separate scene is required for the first action of Act 2 involving Romeo, Mercutio, and Benvolio. In the Garrick-Kemble text this scene is labeled as taking place in *An Open Place, adjoining Capulet's Garden*; the effect is presumably created by means of grooved flats pushed onstage from the wings. Once Mercutio and Benvolio go off, having concluded that Romeo is nowhere to be found, we are introduced to a new scene in Garrick-Kemble: *Capulet's Garden*. A stage direction specifies that Juliet *"appears at a Balcony, and sits down."* Thereafter, the love conference of Romeo and Juliet proceeds much as in Shakespeare.

Another significant transformation of stage space occurs in Act 3, when Romeo, now banished for having slain Tybalt, and having consummated his marriage with Juliet in their one brief night together, must say farewell to her.

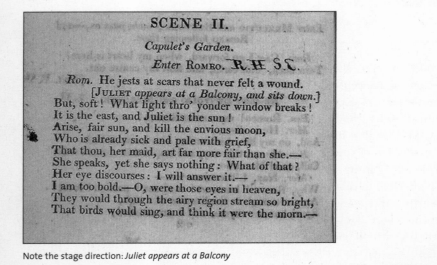

SCENE II.

Capulet's Garden.

Enter ROMEO. R. H. S.

Rom. He jests at scars that never felt a wound.
      [JULIET *appears at a Balcony, and sits down.*]
But, soft! What light thro' yonder window breaks!
It is the east, and Juliet is the sun!
Arise, fair sun, and kill the envious moon,
Who is already sick and pale with grief,
That thou, her maid, art far more fair than she.——
She speaks, yet she says nothing: What of that?
Her eye discourses: I will answer it.——
I am too bold.——O, were those eyes in heaven,
They would through the airy region stream so bright,
That birds would sing, and think it were the morn.——

Note the stage direction: *Juliet appears at a Balcony*

In Shakespeare's script, they are *"aloft,"* that is to say, in the gallery rear stage that earlier represented Juliet's window. The script makes much of Romeo's descent from this gallery, by rope ladder, in full view of the audience. After he has departed, Shakespeare then arranges for Juliet to come down behind the scenes to the main stage in order that the ensuing long scene of confrontation with her father, mother, and Nurse over the proposed marriage to Count Paris can be acted out on the main stage; the gallery is too constricted a space for this large scene. The result is that a single continuous scene is acted in two locations, above in the gallery and then below on the main stage. Garrick-Kemble's strategy is more literal and representational, in accord with eighteenth-century ideas of decorum about stage representation. Romeo and Juliet are never *"aloft"* in this sequence; they bid a tearful farewell to each other in Capulet's Garden, on the main stage. Then, in a separate scene identified by new flats, labeled *Juliet's Chamber* and then rechristened *Juliet's Antechamber* by an annotator of the promptbook, Juliet confronts her parents and her nurse.

In Act 4, when Juliet swallows the potion that Friar Laurence has given her and falls into a deep sleep on her bed, Garrick and Kemble again alter the staging. Shakespeare clearly calls for a stage arrangement in which the curtained four-poster bed is onstage (having been thrust out from behind the scenes) and is thus visible throughout the ensuing action as her family members prepare for the wedding that we know will never take place. She is there when the nurse comes to attempt without success to awaken her. The visual juxtaposition is striking and ironic, since we are aware of Juliet's silent presence throughout. Garrick and Kemble, bound by the conventions of verisimilitude, choose instead to present separate scenes; they move back and forth from *A Room in Capulet's House* to *Juliet's Bedchamber*. The choice is absolutely characteristic of the ways in which the eighteenth and early nineteenth centuries strove to "improve" Shakespeare's staging.

In the final churchyard scene, as indicated above, Juliet awakens before Romeo dies of poison—long enough before that death, in fact, that the lovers can perform quite a death scene between them (see pages 316-319). The verses here, newly devised for the occasion, are based on Matteo Bandello's *Novelle* (1554) to which Shakespeare was ultimately indebted (though his immediate source was Arthur Brooke's long poem, *The Tragical History of Romeus and Juliet*, 1562, in which Romeo dies as in Shakespeare's play). Romeo actually brings Juliet forth from the tomb before she realizes who it is that has wakened her. The dialogue continues for some sixty-four lines, as Romeo explains to her that he has taken poison, supposing her to have died. Once Romeo is dead, Juliet faints on his body, and does not stir until Friar Laurence has come to urge that she leave the tomb. In the final moments of this Garrick-Kemble adaptation, Friar Laurence does not recount to the Prince and others what has happened, as he does in Shakespeare's text; the ending is shortened considerably to leave the audience the awesome impact of the sad ending of the two lovers. The ending is thus in keeping with the spirit of the Garrick-Kemble enterprise throughout. It magnifies the roles of the lovers, enhances their trueness to each other, and gives them a central position in the final stage picture. This production is, from first to last, a quintessential product of the age for which it was devised.

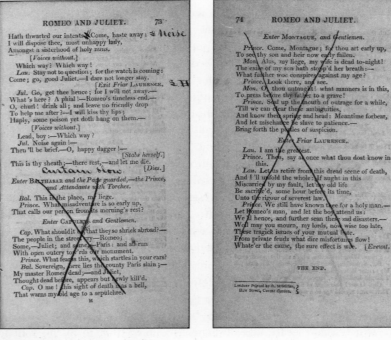

Garrick and Kemble's shortened ending

"What's in a name?":

Romeo and Juliet AND POP CULTURE

Douglas Lanier

None of Shakespeare's plays has had a more lasting or ubiquitous effect in popular culture than *Romeo and Juliet*. This might seem rather odd, since his later tragedies—*Hamlet, Macbeth, King Lear, Julius Caesar,* and *Othello*—are generally regarded by scholars as more accomplished and sophisticated plays. But the enormous influence of *Romeo and Juliet* becomes less surprising when one realizes how much pop music, literature, and film is devoted to the joys and vexations of romance and how fully Shakespeare's popular reputation as the poet of love rests upon this one early tragedy. It is a telling fact that of all the film adaptations of Shakespeare's plays, only those of *Romeo and Juliet* have been consistent commercial successes at the box office.

In particular the balcony scene has become an instantly recognizable image for romantic devotion (and, indeed, for all of Shakespearean theater), a favorite point of popular reference often detached from its original dramatic context and reproduced in all manner of popular media and genres. The sheer range of media, contexts, and cultures in which versions of this scene appear is overwhelming: it makes cameos in candy bar and mobile phone advertisements, variety radio shows, TV sitcoms, romance novels, adventure comic books, film Westerns, animated series, musicals, operas, and children's programs, to name but a very few. In some cases, the balcony scene is not merely an image of romance but its catalyst.

One recurring motif of works directed to young readers is that of the school production of *Romeo and Juliet* in which young actors playing Romeo and Juliet use the balcony scene to express obliquely their unspoken attraction to each other; this motif appears with some regularity in Japanese *manga*, most notably in Rumiko Takahashi's popular *Ranma*. Versions of this motif also feature prominently in the entertaining silent film *Doubling for Romeo* (Clarence Badger, 1921), which chronicles the attempts of a Hollywood stuntman (played by Will Rogers) to learn from Shakespeare's play the proper way to woo his sweetheart, and, more recently, in an episode of the popular teen sitcom *Beverly Hills 90210* ("Summer Storm").

ICONIC SCENE

The very ubiquity and familiarity of the balcony scene makes it an irresistible object for lampoon. At times, the parodic focus falls on the high seriousness of the scene or quality of the acting, replaying it as farce, as in the minstrel parody "Pay as You Exit," a 1936 *Little Rascals* short that casts Buckwheat as a blonde-wigged Juliet in a comically disastrous amateur production (it targets MGM's lavish film production released in the same year). In the film *Panic Button* (George Sherman, 1964), an equally miscast Jayne Mansfield and Maurice Chevalier butcher the balcony scene as part of a scheme to create an intentionally doomed television pilot, a plotline that predates *The Producers* by four years. Popular burlesques of the balcony scene often target Shakespeare's ornate language. Indeed, the balcony scene first appears in talking pictures in *The Hollywood Revue of 1929* (Charles Reisner, 1929) as a comedy vignette: stars John Gilbert and Norma Shearer at first play the scene "straight," then immediately reperform it in silly jazz-age jargon and pig latin. Parodies of the balcony scene have been a particular favorite among Anglo-American animators, cartoonists, and puppeteers. Popeye and Olive Oyl, Mickey Mouse and company, Bugs Bunny, the Flintstones, Archie, the Animaniacs, the Muppets, and the Smurfs, among many others, have all starred in burlesques of the scene. The forthcoming Disney musical *Gnomeo and Juliet* (due in 2006) promises to extend that sort of cartoon parody to the computer animation age. Eastern European animators, by contrast, have tended to favor serio-comic treatments of *Romeo and Juliet*, often showcasing innovative animation techniques and adding allegorical political subtexts, as in Bob Calinescu's *Romeo si Julieta* (1968) and Dusan Petrovic's *Romeo and Juliet* (1984).

Equally iconic are the lines that Romeo and Juliet exchange in this scene, particularly Juliet's "Romeo, Romeo, wherefore art thou Romeo?," a line widely misunderstood ("wherefore" means not "where" but "why") that appears in pop contexts both serious and parodic. A gag in the pilot episode of *Joey*, a spinoff of the hit TV series *Friends*, is typical of comedy built upon the misrecognition of Shakespeare's lines. To impress a potential date, Joey, a dim-witted actor, recites his audition piece "Romeo, Romeo, wherefore art thou Romeo?," only to pulled up short when the woman reminds him that these are Juliet's, not Romeo's lines. Indeed, the very over-familiarity of Romeo and Juliet's declarations of love can become the stuff of popular comedy. In *Time Flies* (Walter Forde, 1944), when a time-traveling showgirl encounters Shakespeare struggling to write the balcony scene, she, already knowing the bard's monumental text from the future, supplies the playwright with the lines he is always destined to have written, in the process correcting some of Shakespeare's own less felicitous alternatives. A similar joke runs throughout the surprise hit film *Shakespeare in Love* (John Madden, 1999), in which Will Shakespeare wrestles with his awful play-in-draft, *Romeo and Ethel, the Pirate's Daughter*, before meeting his muse, Viola de Lessups, and crafting his first masterpiece *Romeo and Juliet*. Shakespeare's balcony scene, we come to recognize, is Will's idealized reimagining of his and Viola's comically disastrous meeting outside Viola's window. Later, in one of the film's most remarkable sequences, the two lovers run the lines of Will's freshly-penned balcony scene to each other in bed (with the genders reversed), against which is intercut a cross-dressed rehearsal of the same scene in the theater. The effect is both romantic and parodic. Will and Viola's rehearsal emphasizes the erotic subtext of the lines and brings the scene in line with the conventions of contemporary romance—in Shakespeare's play, the balcony scene is about delay, not consummation—while at the same time we are reminded of the couple's earlier farcical introduction and the artificial nature (to modern tastes) of Renaissance theatrical practice. In addition to these motifs, *Shakespeare in Love* wittily exemplifies yet another ubiquitous impulse in pop adaptation of Shakespeare: imagining the biographical origins that lie behind Shakespeare's fictional creations, this even though nearly all of Shakespeare's plays are demonstrably theatrical adaptations of prior sources, in this case, of Arthur Brooke's *The Tragical History of Romeus and Juliet* (1562).

ENDURING PLOTLINE: YOUNG LOVE

More generally, *Romeo and Juliet* has provided one of the most enduring plotlines for pop depictions of romance: love between two youths blocked by some conflict between two older generations or social groups. Whether *Romeo and Juliet* is the direct source for these plotlines or merely yet another example of a long-lived, cross-cultural narrative of blocked romance is an interesting question for debate. Writers have recast the conflict at the heart of this plotline in seemingly endless variations, from the profound to the trivial—to offer a sampling see the following list:

Modern-day Romeos and Juliets

Irish unionists and separatists	Joan Lingard's young adult novel series begun with *The Twelfth Day of July* (1997) Ben Elton's soccer musical, *The Beautiful Game* (1999) Andrew Lloyd Webber and Mary McGuckian's film *This is the Sea* (1997)
Indian and British	James Merchant's *Shakespeare Wallah* (1965)
Cold War Russians and Americans	Peter Ustinov's play and film *Romanoff and Juliet* (1961)
blacks and immigrant Indians in the deep South	Mira Nair's *Mississippi Masala* (1991)
law enforcers and pornographers	Jim Leonard's Fox TV series *Skin* (2003)
rival food-stand operators	Chee Kong Cheah's film *The Chicken Rice War* (2000)
valley girls and city punkers	Martha Coolidge's film *Valley Girl* (1983)
mutants and normals	Marvel Comics' *Uncanny X-Men Volume 5: She Lies with Angels* (2004)

Even though Shakespeare's version pointedly never reveals the origin of the antagonism between the Montagues and Capulets, in pop adaptations of the play the source of conflict between families is often specified and has become a well-worn device for commenting on social conflict and prejudice. Accordingly, Shakespeare's tale of blocked romance has had an especially vigorous afterlife in those cultures where arranged marriage or strict parental or family honor remain active facts of life. Films of the Indian subcontinent, for example, quite frequently use *Romeo and Juliet*-like scenarios as their basic armature, and the motif is made prominent in Egyptian, Japanese, Korean, Middle Eastern and Eastern European film and stage versions of the play. In light of recent controversies over gay rights and the prominence of *Romeo and Juliet* as an icon of heterosexual romance, it is interesting to note the emergence of gay reimaginings of Shakespeare's plotline, seen in such films as the adult film musical *Romeo and Julian* (Sam Abdul, 1993), Joe Calarco's play *R&J*, and the daring French Guinea film *Dakan* (Mohamed Camara, 1997). Related to the interest in conflict between families or social groups is the drive in many pop versions of this plotline to imagine some sort of happy ending for Romeo and Juliet, a means for rising above, resolving or avoiding the tragic fate that envelopes Shakespeare's lovers. Many of the versions mentioned above end happily rather than tragically, and those that do not often emphasize the chastening effect of the lovers' sufferings. This drive toward comedy has sparked a subgenre of pop works that imagine the next frame out of the *Romeo and Juliet* story, the lovers married and, in parodic versions, living not so happily ever after. The ending of the exploitation parody *Tromeo and Juliet* (Lloyd Kaufmann, 1996) has it both ways: instead of dying for love, Tromeo and Juliet (who, we learn, are brother and sister) marry for lust, move to the New Jersey suburbs, and raise their mutant children in the shadow of nearby chemical plants.

This change in connotation points to perhaps the most important shift in popular understanding of the *Romeo and Juliet* story: its strong identification with youth culture. In the course of the century, Romeo and Juliet have definitively become teenagers, pitted against an older generation who stands in the way of their romantic fulfillment and independence. One can trace this change most easily by observing the ages of the actors playing the lovers in the major mass-market films of the play:

ROMEO AND JULIET THROUGH THE AGES

Production	Romeo	Juliet
George Cukor, 1936	Leslie Howard, 43	Norma Shearer, 34
Renato Castellani, 1954	Laurence Harvey, 26	Susan Shentall, 20
Franco Zeffirelli, 1968	Leonard Whiting, 18	Olivia Hussey, 17
Baz Luhrmann, 1996	Leonardo DiCaprio, 22	Claire Danes, 17

Indeed, both Zeffirelli and Luhrmann's films redefined Romeo and Juliet as youth culture icons for their respective generations. Zeffirelli's Romeo was a pacifistic romantic dreamer and his Juliet a plucky flower child, both appropriate for the "make love, not war" 60s, while Luhrmann presented his Romeo and Juliet as disaffected Gen-Xers disillusioned with their corporate establishment parents and surrounded by media commercialism, casual violence, and empty religious iconography. However, the adaptation which most cemented the identification of *Romeo and Juliet* with youth culture was the 1957 musical *West Side Story*, subsequently filmed in 1961 by Robert Wise. *West Side Story* transposed Shakespeare's plot to the urban gang culture of New York City, taking up the contemporary social issues of juvenile delinquency and racial tension, a relatively new focus for the musical. The film magnified that sense of grittiness and immediacy by filming many dance sequences on the streets of New York rather than a sound stage. But much of *West Side Story*'s appeal springs from its extraordinary dance sequences choreographed by Jerome Robbins and the inventive score by Leonard Bernstein, which deftly straddles the line between classical music, jazz, and pop. Indeed, it is a measure of the musical's importance that it has itself spawned a subgenre, the "street" adaptation of *Romeo and Juliet*, a subgenre which includes, in addition to Luhrmann's film, works as diverse as the Eastern European rock opera *Meile ir mirtis Veronoje* (*Love and Death in Verona*), Rennie Harris Puremovement's hip-hop dance piece *Rome and Jewels*, Abel Ferrara's film *China Girl*, Gideon Sams's novel *The Punk* (later made by Michael Sarne into the film *The Punk and the Princess*), and Ren Savant's pornographic epic *Westside*. The close identification of the lovers with contemporary youth culture does much to explain the frequency of allusions to *Romeo and Juliet* in pop music and film. In the 90s, the commercial success of Luhrmann's *Romeo + Juliet* also sparked the hope that other literary classics might be profitably reshaped for the youth market, resulting in a flurry of teen and twenty-something film adaptations of Shakespeare plays. This popular identification has also reshaped dominant interpretations of *Romeo and Juliet*: no longer seen as tragic casualties of fate or their own ill-considered haste, the lovers are now most often presented as innocent victims of social prejudice or a callous older generation.

IN REALITY

Like so many of Shakespeare's characters, Romeo and Juliet have taken on a quasi-historical reality that belies their fictional nature. A balcony designated as Juliet's has become a tourist attraction in Verona, and at one time, letters addressed to Juliet in Verona were answered by a local professor. The latter formed the inspiration for Elvis Costello's unusual song-cycle project, *The Juliet Letters*, which set texts supposedly written to and from Juliet to moody string quartet accompaniment. Imagining the voice of one of the lovers is also the burden of the witty song "Here in Heaven" by the group Sparks (on *Kimono my House*), which pictures Romeo looking down from heaven to discover that Juliet is not dead after all.

Romeo and Juliet have also entered the pantheon of those Shakespearean characters whose names now identify general character-types rather than specific individuals, particularly when those names are used in popular song, titles of popular literature, and journalism. "Romeo," for example, has popularly come to designate a male romantic of any sort. However, as scholar Stephen Buhler has demonstrated, the connotations of the names "Romeo" and "Juliet" in popular song have changed over time. In the early twentieth-century pop culture, "Romeo" often designated an older lothario and "Juliet" a romantic innocent, but in the course of the century the dominant connotation of the two names changed, "Romeo" becoming a younger, more dreamy and romantic type and "Juliet" a more self-possessed young woman. It is possible that popular connotations attached to the character "Romeo" may change yet again as a result of citations in rap music and hip-hop productions, where the name often designates a macho sexual player rather than a sensitive romancer of women, in effect returning "Romeo" to an earlier popular sense of the type.

Dramatis Personae

ESCALUS, prince of Verona

PARIS, a young nobleman, kinsman to the prince

MONTAGUE,
CAPULET } heads of two houses at variance with each other

An old man, cousin to Capulet

ROMEO, son to Montague

MERCUTIO, kinsman to the prince and friend to Romeo

BENVOLIO, nephew to Montague, and friend to Romeo

TYBALT, nephew to Lady Capulet

FRIAR LAURENCE,
FRIAR JOHN } Franciscans

BALTHASAR, servant to Romeo

SAMPSON,
GREGORY } servants to Capulet

PETER, servant to Juliet's nurse

ABRAHAM, servant to Montague

An APOTHECARY

Three Musicians

Page to Paris; another Page; an officer

LADY MONTAGUE, wife to Montague

LADY CAPULET, wife to Capulet

JULIET, daughter to Capulet

NURSE to Juliet

Citizens of Verona: several Men and Women, relations to both houses,
Maskers, Guards, Watchmen, and Attendants

Chorus

[Romeo and Juliet

Prologue

1: **dignity**: worth and social standing

3: **mutiny**: discord

6: **star-crossed:** not favored by the stars, unfortunate

7: **misadventured**: unfortunate

12: **two hours' traffic of our stage:** subject of our two-hour play

track 21

1–14:
Andrew Wade with members of the Guthrie Experience for Actors in Training

The Prologue]

CHORUS

Two households, both alike in dignity,
(In fair Verona where we lay our scene),
From ancient grudge break to new mutiny,
Where civil blood makes civil hands unclean.
From forth the fatal loins of these two foes   5
A pair of star-crossed lovers take their life;
Whose misadventured piteous overthrows
Doth with their death bury their parents' strife.
The fearful passage of their death-marked love,
And the continuance of their parents' rage,   10
Which, but their children's end, nought could remove,
Is now the two hours' traffic of our stage.
The which if you with patient ears attend,
What here shall miss, our toil shall strive to mend.

[Romeo and Juliet

Act 1

Stage direction: **bucklers:** shields

1: **carry coals:** to put up with insults

2: **colliers:** 1) diggers or sellers of coals 2) very dirty; also implies dirty in reputation

3: **choler:** anger, with a pun on both "collar" and "collier"

4: **draw:** i.e., draw our swords

4: **collar:** i.e., hangman's noose

10: **take the wall:** get the better of

12: **weakest goes to the wall:** i.e., in fights, the weakest must yield to the strong (proverbial)

J. P. Kemble, in his 1814 production at the Theatres Royal, gave Sampson's lines to Peter, the Nurse's Servant.

Act 1: Scene 1]

[Enter SAMPSON and GREGORY, of the house of Capulet,
armed with swords and bucklers]

SAMPSON
　Gregory, on my word, we'll not carry coals.

GREGORY
　No, for then we should be colliers.

SAMPSON
　I mean, an we be in choler, we'll draw.

GREGORY
　Ay, while you live, draw your neck out of collar.

SAMPSON
　I strike quickly, being moved.   5

GREGORY
　But thou art not quickly moved to strike.

SAMPSON
　A dog of the house of Montague moves me.

GREGORY
　To move is to stir, and to be valiant is to stand. Therefore, if thou art
　moved, thou runn'st away.

SAMPSON
　A dog of that house shall move me to stand. I will take the wall   10
　of any man or maid of Montague's.

GREGORY
　That shows thee a weak slave, for the weakest goes to the wall.

13–14: **thrust to the wall:** a sexual reference

14: **from the wall:** i.e., be superior to them

15: **to the wall:** i.e., make love to them (sets up the string of sexual references that follow)

20: **maidenheads:** virginity

Costume design for Peter, a Capulet servant, in John Gielgud's 1935 production
Rare Book and Special Collections Library, University of Illinois at Urbana-Champaign

25: **poor John:** salted hake (a type of poor fare)

SAMPSON
'Tis true, and therefore women, being the weaker vessels, are ever thrust
to the wall. Therefore I will push Montague's men from the wall and
thrust his maids to the wall.   15

GREGORY
The quarrel is between our masters and us their men.

SAMPSON
'Tis all one. I will show myself a tyrant. When I have fought with the
men, I will be civil with the maids; I will cut off their heads.

GREGORY
The heads of the maids?

SAMPSON
Ay, the heads of the maids, or their maidenheads; take it in what   20
sense thou wilt.

GREGORY
They must take it in sense that feel it.

SAMPSON
Me they shall feel while I am able to stand, and 'tis known I am a pretty
piece of flesh.

GREGORY
'Tis well thou art not fish; if thou hadst, thou hadst been poor John.   25
Draw thy tool. Here comes two of the house of the Montagues.
                                    [*Enter two other servingmen*]

SAMPSON
My naked weapon is out. Quarrel, I will back thee.

GREGORY
How? Turn thy back and run?

SAMPSON
Fear me not.

30: **marry:** indeed, to be sure

31: **take the law of our sides:** have justice on our side

33: **bite my thumb at them:** an insult performed by putting the nail of the thumb between the teeth and flicking it towards one's opponent

Costume design for Montague servants in John Gielgud's 1935 production
Rare Book and Special Collections Library, University of Illinois at Urbana-Champaign

GREGORY
No, marry; I fear thee. 30

SAMPSON
Let us take the law of our sides; let them begin.

GREGORY
I will frown as I pass by, and let them take it as they list.

SAMPSON
Nay, as they dare, I will bite my thumb at them, which is a disgrace to them if they bear it.

[*Enter ABRAHAM and BALTHASAR*]

ABRAHAM
Do you bite your thumb at us, sir? 35

SAMPSON
I do bite my thumb, sir.

ABRAHAM
Do you bite your thumb at us, sir?

SAMPSON
[*Aside to GREGORY*] Is the law of our side if I say "Ay"?

GREGORY
No.

SAMPSON
No, sir, I do not bite my thumb at you, sir, but I bite my thumb, sir. 40

GREGORY
Do you quarrel, sir?

ABRAHAM
Quarrel sir? No, sir.

49: **swashing:** smashing

52: **heartless hinds:** cowardly servants
(heartless = wanting courage; hinds = servants)

> 6   ROMEO AND JULIET.
>
> *Gre.* Do you quarrel, sir?
> *Bal.* Quarrel, sir? no, sir.
> *Sam.* If you do, sir, I am for you; I serve as good
> a man as you.
> *Bal.* No better, sir.
> *Sam.* Well, sir.
> *Gre.* Say—better; here comes one of my master's
> kinsmen.
> *Sam.* Yes, better, sir.
> *Bal.* You lie.
> *Sam.* Draw, if you be men.—Gregory, remember
> thy swashing blow.—[*They fight.*]
>   *Enter* BENVOLIO.
>
> *Ben.* Part, fools; put up your swords; you know
> not what you do.—[*Beats down their weapons.*]
>   *Enter* TYBALT, *with his sword drawn.*
>
> *Tyb.* What, art thou drawn among these heartless
>   hinds?
> Turn thee, Benvolio; look upon thy death.
> *Ben.* I do but keep the peace; put up thy sword;
> Or manage it, to part these men, with me.
> *Tyb.* What, drawn, and talk of peace? I hate the
>   word
> As I hate hell, all Montagues, and thee:
> Have at thee, coward.—[*They fight.*]
>   [C͟a͟p͟u͟l͟e͟t͟s͟ ͟a͟n͟d͟ M͟o͟n͟t͟a͟g͟u͟e͟s͟ ͟w͟i͟t͟h͟o͟u͟t͟.]
> M͟o͟n͟t͟a͟g͟u͟e͟s͟.͟—͟D͟o͟w͟n͟ ͟w͟i͟t͟h͟ ͟t͟h͟e͟ ͟C͟a͟p͟u͟l͟e͟t͟s͟!
> C͟a͟p͟u͟l͟e͟t͟s͟.͟—͟D͟o͟w͟n͟ ͟w͟i͟t͟h͟ ͟t͟h͟e͟ ͟M͟o͟n͟t͟a͟g͟u͟e͟s͟!
>   [*Bell rings.*]
>   [CAPULET *without.*]
> *Cap.* Give me my sword! Old Montague is come,
> And flourishes his blade in spite of me.
> *Enter* MONTAGUE a͟n͟d͟ ͟h͟i͟s͟ ͟F͟r͟i͟e͟n͟d͟s͟, *and* CAPULET w͟i͟t͟h͟
>   h͟i͟s͟ ͟F͟r͟i͟e͟n͟d͟s͟, ͟a͟l͟l͟ ͟a͟r͟m͟e͟d͟.
>
> *Mon.* Thou villain, Capulet,——[T͟h͟e͟y͟ ͟a͟l͟l͟ ͟f͟i͟g͟h͟t͟.]

J. P. Kemble's 1814 production left the fight in but cut out most of the crowd,
leaving the key players as combatants.

SAMPSON
But if you do, sir, I am for you. I serve as good a man as you.

ABRAHAM
No better.

SAMPSON
Well, sir.   45
[Enter BENVOLIO]

GREGORY
Say "better"; here comes one of my master's kinsmen.

SAMPSON
Yes, better, sir.

ABRAHAM
You lie.

SAMPSON
Draw if you be men. Gregory, remember thy swashing blow.
[They fight]

BENVOLIO
Part, fools!   50
Put up your swords. You know not what you do.
[Enter TYBALT]

TYBALT
What, art thou drawn among these heartless hinds?
Turn thee, Benvolio; look upon thy death.

BENVOLIO
I do but keep the peace. Put up thy sword,
Or manage it to part these men with me.   55

TYBALT
What, drawn, and talk of peace? I hate the word
As I hate hell, all Montagues, and thee.
Have at thee, coward!

62: **crutch:** Lady Capulet suggest that a crutch would be more suitable than a sword for a man of Lord Capulet's age

64: **in spite of me:** to challenge me

68: **neighbour-stainèd:** stained by the blood of countrymen

73: **mistempered:** manufactured for an evil purpose

[They fight]
[Enter three or four citizens with clubs or partisans]

First Citizen

Clubs, bills, and partisans! Strike! Beat them down!
Down with the Capulets! Down with the Montagues!   60
[Enter old CAPULET, in his gown, and his wife]

CAPULET

What noise is this? Give me my long sword, ho!

LADY CAPULET

A crutch, a crutch! Why call you for a sword?

CAPULET

My sword, I say! Old Montague is come
And flourishes his blade in spite of me.
[Enter old MONTAGUE and his wife]

MONTAGUE

Thou villain, Capulet! — Hold me not; let me go.   65

LADY MONTAGUE

Thou shalt not stir a foot to seek a foe.
[Enter PRINCE Escalus with his train]

PRINCE

Rebellious subjects, enemies to peace,
Profaners of this neighbour-stainèd steel, —
Will they not hear? What, ho! You men, you beasts,
That quench the fire of your pernicious rage   70
With purple fountains issuing from your veins.
On pain of torture from those bloody hands,
Throw your mistempered weapons to the ground,
And hear the sentence of your movèd prince.
Three civil brawls, bred of an airy word   75
By thee, old Capulet, and Montague,
Have thrice disturbed the quiet of our streets
And made Verona's ancient citizens,

79: **grave beseeming:** worthy, sober, dignified

81: **cankered with peace:** made insensitive to peace

81: **cankered hate:** corruption, evil

83: **forfeit of the peace:** penalty or fine for the breach of the peace

90: **set...abroach:** i.e., incited this brawl

98: **withal:** with it, i.e., with Tybalt's sword

100: **on part and part:** one side and the other side (part = side)

Cast by their grave beseeming ornaments,
To wield old partisans in hands as old,   80
Cankered with peace, to part your cankered hate.
If ever you disturb our streets again,
Your lives shall pay the forfeit of the peace.
For this time, all the rest depart away.
You, Capulet, shall go along with me,   85
And Montague, come you this afternoon
To know our further pleasure in this case
To old Free-town, our common judgment-place.
Once more, on pain of death, all men depart.
    [*Exeunt all but MONTAGUE, LADY MONTAGUE, and BENVOLIO*]

MONTAGUE
Who set this ancient quarrel new abroach?   90
Speak, nephew, were you by when it began?

BENVOLIO
Here were the servants of your adversary
And yours, close fighting ere I did approach.
I drew to part them. In the instant came
The fiery Tybalt, with his sword prepared,   95
Which, as he breathed defiance to my ears,
He swung about his head and cut the winds,
Who, nothing hurt withal, hissed him in scorn.
While we were interchanging thrusts and blows
Came more and more and fought on part and part,   100
Till the prince came, who parted either part.

LADY MONTAGUE
O, where is Romeo? Saw you him today?
Right glad I am he was not at this fray.

BENVOLIO
Madam, an hour before the worshipped sun
Peered forth the golden window of the east,   105
A troubled mind drove me to walk abroad
Where, underneath the grove of sycamore
That westward rooteth from this city side,

110: **ware:** aware

122: **Aurora:** goddess of the morning

127: **humour:** disposition, mood

131: **importuned:** pressed, urgently solicited

136: **sounding:** being examined, getting to the bottom of

137: **envious:** malignant

8   ROMEO AND JULIET.

And stole into the covert of the wood :
I, measuring his affections by my own,—
That most are busied when they 're most alone,—
Pursu'd my humour, not pursuing his,
And gladly shunn'd who gladly fled from me.
~~Mon. Many a morning hath he there been seen,~~
~~With tears augmenting the fresh morning's dew ;~~
~~But, all so soon as the all-cheering sun~~
~~Should in the furthest east begin to draw~~
~~The shady curtains from Aurora's bed,~~
~~Away from light steals home my heavy son,~~
~~And private in his chamber pens himself ;~~
~~Shuts up his windows, locks fair daylight out,~~
~~And makes himself an artificial night :~~
Black and portentous must this humour prove,
Unless good counsel may the cause remove.
  Ben. My noble uncle, do you know the cause ?
  Mon. I neither know it, nor can learn it of him.
  Ben. Have you importun'd him by any means ?
  Mon. Both by myself and many other friends :
~~But he, his own affections' counsellor,~~
~~Is to himself—I will not say, how true—~~
~~But to himself so secret and so close,~~
~~So far from sounding and discovery,~~
~~As is the bud bit with an envious worm,~~
~~Ere he can spread his sweet leaves to the air,~~
~~Or dedicate his beauty to the sun.~~
  Ben. So please you, sir, Mercutio and myself
Are most near to him ;—be it that our years,
Births, fortunes, studies, inclinations,
Measure the rule of his, I know not ; but
Friendship still loves to sort him with his like ;—
We will attempt upon his privacy :
And could we learn from whence his sorrows grow
We would as willingly give cure, as knowledge.
  Mon. 'T will bind us to you : Good Benvolio, go.
  Ben. We 'll know his grievance, or be much denied.
                                   [Exeunt.

J. P. Kemble has excised Rosaline from this production. Thus, he cuts details of Romeo's melancholy, suggesting vague moodiness instead of lovesickness.

So early walking did I see your son.
Towards him I made, but he was ware of me   110
And stole into the covert of the wood.
I, measuring his affections by my own,
Which then most sought where most might not be found,
Being one too many by my weary self,
Pursued my humour, not pursuing his,   115
And gladly shunned who gladly fled from me.

MONTAGUE
Many a morning hath he there been seen,
With tears augmenting the fresh morning dew,
Adding to clouds more clouds with his deep sighs;
But all so soon, as the all-cheering sun   120
Should in the farthest east begin to draw
The shady curtains from Aurora's bed,
Away from the light steals home my heavy son,
And private in his chamber pens himself,
Shuts up his windows, locks fair daylight out   125
And makes himself an artificial night.
Black and portentous must this humour prove,
Unless good counsel may the cause remove.

BENVOLIO
My noble uncle, do you know the cause?

MONTAGUE
I neither know it nor can learn of him.   130

BENVOLIO
Have you importuned him by any means?

MONTAGUE
Both by myself and many other friends.
But he, his own affections' counsellor,
Is to himself — I will not say how true —
But to himself so secret and so close,   135
So far from sounding and discovery,
As is the bud bit with an envious worm,

145: **shrift:** confession made to a priest and the absolution consequent upon it

146: **morrow:** morning

Line 146: "Good-morrow, cousin": John Harrison as Benvolio (back turned)
finds a melancholic and contemplative Romeo, played by Laurence Payne
Photo: Royal Shakespeare Company (1947)

Ere he can spread his sweet leaves to the air
Or dedicate his beauty to the sun.
Could we but learn from whence his sorrows grow.   140
We would as willingly give cure as know.

[*Enter ROMEO*]

BENVOLIO
See, where he comes. So please you, step aside;
I'll know his grievance or be much denied.

MONTAGUE
I would thou wert so happy by thy stay,
To hear true shrift. Come, madam, let's away.   145
[*Exeunt MONTAGUE and LADY MONTAGUE*]

BENVOLIO
Good-morrow, cousin.

ROMEO
                        Is the day so young?

BENVOLIO
But new struck nine.

ROMEO
                        Ay me, sad hours seem long.
Was that my father that went hence so fast?   150

BENVOLIO
It was. What sadness lengthens Romeo's hours?

ROMEO
Not having that, which, having, makes them short.

BENVOLIO
In love?

ROMEO
Out —

158: **tyrannous:** cruel, pitiless

159: **muffled still:** blindfolded always ("Love is blind")

167: **well-seeming:** having a good appearance

169: **still-waking:** silent, calm and quiet

172: **coz:** a contraction of cousin

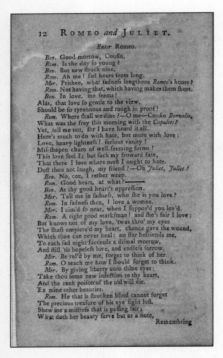

In Garrick's production, on which J. P. Kemble's is based, Romeo's melancholy and early morning wanderings are left in. However, Benvolio's speech is reworked, and the rest of the scene, featuring him discussing Rosaline with Romeo, has been moved to after 1.3. Furthermore, the girl over whom Romeo is lovesick is no longer Rosaline, but Juliet!

BENVOLIO
    Of love?   155

ROMEO
    Out of her favour, where I am in love.

BENVOLIO
    Alas, that love, so gentle in his view,
    Should be so tyrannous and rough in proof.

ROMEO
    Alas, that love, whose view is muffled still,
    Should, without eyes, see pathways to his will.   160
    Where shall we dine? O me! What fray was here?
    Yet tell me not, for I have heard it all.
    Here's much to do with hate, but more with love.
    Why, then, O brawling love, O loving hate,
    O any thing, of nothing first create.   165
    O heavy lightness, serious vanity,
    Misshapen chaos of well-seeming forms,
    Feather of lead, bright smoke, cold fire, sick health,
    Still-waking sleep that is not what it is.
    This love feel I that feel no love in this.   170
    Dost thou not laugh?

BENVOLIO
                        No, coz, I rather weep.

ROMEO
    Good heart, at what?

BENVOLIO
                    At thy good heart's oppression.

ROMEO
    Why, such is love's transgression.   175
    Griefs of mine own lie heavy in my breast,
    Which thou wilt propagate, to have it prest
    With more of thine. This love that thou hast shown

184: **choking gall:** something bitter and disagreeable

184: **preserving sweet:** something agreeable and luscious to the taste

186: **soft:** stay, stop

190: **sadness:** seriousness

198: **right fair mark:** clear target

Doth add more grief to too much of mine own.
Love is a smoke raised with the fume of sighs;   180
Being purged, a fire sparkling in lovers' eyes;
Being vexed a sea nourished with loving tears.
What is it else? A madness most discreet,
A choking gall, and a preserving sweet.
Farewell, my coz.   185

BENVOLIO
              Soft, I will go along.
An if you leave me so, you do me wrong.

ROMEO
Tut, I have lost myself; I am not here.
This is not Romeo, he's some other where.

BENVOLIO
Tell me in sadness, who is that you love?   190

ROMEO
What, shall I groan and tell thee?

BENVOLIO
Groan? Why, no. But sadly, tell me who.

ROMEO
A sick man in sadness make his will;
A word ill urged to one that is so ill.
In sadness, cousin, I do love a woman.   195

BENVOLIO
I aimed so near when I supposed you loved.

ROMEO
A right good markman, and she's fair I love.

BENVOLIO
A right fair mark, fair coz, is soonest hit.

200: **Dian's wit:** Dian = Diana, the goddess of the moon and of chastity; wit = intellectual power

203: **stay the siege:** withstand the attack

213: **merit bliss:** deserve the highest degree of happiness

ROMEO

 Well, in that hit you miss. She'll not be hit
 With Cupid's arrow. She hath Dian's wit,   200
 And, in strong proof of chastity well armed,
 From love's weak childish bow she lives uncharmed.
 She will not stay the siege of loving terms,
 Nor bide the encounter of assailing eyes,
 Nor ope her lap to saint-seducing gold.   205
 O, she is rich in beauty, only poor
 That when she dies, with beauty dies her store.

BENVOLIO

 Then she hath sworn that she will still live chaste?

ROMEO

 She hath, and in that sparing, makes huge waste,
 For beauty starved with her severity   210
 Cuts beauty off from all posterity.
 She is too fair, too wise, wisely too fair,
 To merit bliss by making me despair.
 She hath forsworn to love, and in that vow
 Do I live dead that live to tell it now.   215

BENVOLIO

 Be ruled by me; forget to think of her.

ROMEO

 O, teach me how I should forget to think.

BENVOLIO

 By giving liberty unto thine eyes;
 Examine other beauties.

ROMEO

      'Tis the way   220
 To call hers exquisite, in question more.
 These happy masks that kiss fair ladies' brows,
 Being black, put us in mind they hide the fair.
 He that is strucken blind cannot forget

Anthony Powell as Benvolio and Derek D. Smith as Romeo in The Shakespeare
Theatre's 1986–1987 production directed by Michael Kahn

Photo: Joan Marcus

230: **I'll pay...die in debt:** I'll teach you or die trying

The precious treasure of his eyesight lost.   225
Show me a mistress that is passing fair;
What doth her beauty serve, but as a note
Where I may read who passed that passing fair?
Farewell. Thou canst not teach me to forget.

BENVOLIO
I'll pay that doctrine, or else die in debt.   230

[Exeunt]

1: **bound:** under bond or legal obligation

Line 1: "But Montague is bound as well as I": C. Aubrey Smith as Lord Capulet and Ralph Forbes as Paris in George Cukor's 1936 movie production
Courtesy: Douglas Lanier

4: **reckoning:** reputation

14: **hopes:** i.e., children

18: **an:** if

18: **her scope of choice:** Juliet's own choices (i.e., the suitors she favors)

20: **accustomed:** customary

Act 1: Scene 2]

CAPULET
    But Montague is bound as well as I,
    In penalty alike, and 'tis not hard, I think,
    For men so old as we to keep the peace.

PARIS
    Of honourable reckoning are you both,
    And pity 'tis you lived at odds so long.   5
    But now, my lord, what say you to my suit?

CAPULET
    But saying o'er what I have said before.
    My child is yet a stranger in the world;
    She hath not seen the change of fourteen years.
    Let two more summers wither in their pride,   10
    Ere we may think her ripe to be a bride.

PARIS
    Younger than she are happy mothers made.

CAPULET
    And too soon marred are those so early made.
    Earth hath swallowed all my hopes but she;
    She's the hopeful lady of my earth.   15
    But woo her, gentle Paris, get her heart.
    My will to her consent is but a part.
    An she agreed, within her scope of choice
    Lies my consent and fair according voice.
    This night I hold an old accustomed feast,   20
    Whereto I have invited many a guest
    Such as I love; and you, among the store,
    One more, most welcome, makes my number more.

25: Earth-treading stars: Capulet is referring to the beautiful women who will be attending his feast

Costume design for party guest in John Gielgud's 1935 production
Rare Book and Special Collections Library, University of Illinois at Urbana-Champaign

47: holp: the old past tense and participle of *help*

·51: **plaintain leaf:** from the herb plantago which is supposed to have great efficacy in healing wounds

At my poor house look to behold this night
Earth-treading stars that make dark heaven light.   25
Such comfort as do lusty young men feel
When well-apparelled April on the heel
Of limping winter treads, even such delight
Among fresh female buds shall you this night
Inherit at my house. Hear all, all see,   30
And like her most whose merit most shall be,
Which one more view of many, mine being one,
May stand in number, though in reck'ning none,
Come, go with me.

                              [To Servant, giving a paper]
             Go, sirrah, trudge about   35
Through fair Verona. Find those persons out
Whose names are written there, and to them say,
My house and welcome, on their pleasure stay.

                      [Exeunt CAPULET and PARIS]

Servant

Find them out whose names are written. Here it is written that
the shoemaker should meddle with his yard, and the tailor with   40
his last, the fisher with his pencil, and the painter with his nets.
But I am sent to find those persons whose names are here writ,
and can never find what names the writing person hath here writ
(I must to the learned) in good time.

                    [Enter BENVOLIO and ROMEO]

BENVOLIO

Tut, man, one fire burns out another's burning,   45
One pain is lessened by another's anguish.
Turn giddy, and be holp by backward turning.
One desperate grief cures with another's languish.
Take thou some new infection to thy eye,
And the rank poison of the old will die.   50

ROMEO

Your plaintain leaf is excellent for that.

BENVOLIO

For what, I pray thee?

57: **God-den:** good evening

Line 64: "Stay, fellow; I can read": Reginald Denny as Benvolio, Leslie Howard as Romeo, and Andy Devine as Peter in George Cukor's 1936 movie production
Courtesy: Douglas Lanier

70: **whither:** where

ROMEO

For your broken shin.

BENVOLIO

Why, Romeo, art thou mad?

ROMEO

Not mad, but bound more than a madman is,   55
Shut up in prison, kept without my food,
Whipped and tormented and — God-den, good fellow.

Servant

God gi' god-den. I pray, sir, can you read?

ROMEO

Ay, mine own fortune in my misery.

Servant

Perhaps you have learned it without book. But, I   60
pray, can you read any thing you see?

ROMEO

Ay, if I know the letters and the language.

Servant

Ye say honestly; rest you merry.

ROMEO

Stay, fellow; I can read.

                                                    [*Reads*]
"Signior Martino and his wife and daughters; County Anselme and   65
his beauteous sisters; the lady widow of Vitravio; Signior
Placentio and his lovely nieces; Mercutio and his brother Valentine;
mine uncle Capulet, his wife and daughters; my fair niece Rosaline;
Livia; Signior Valentio and his cousin Tybalt, Lucio and the lively
Helena." A fair assembly. Whither should they come?   70

Servant

Up.

78–79: **crush a cup of wine:** drink a cup of wine

81: **Rosaline:** In the 1811 Garrick-Kemble production, Romeo is not enamored of a young lady named Rosaline at the start of the play, nor indeed is Rosaline ever mentioned.

83: **unattainted:** not infected, sound

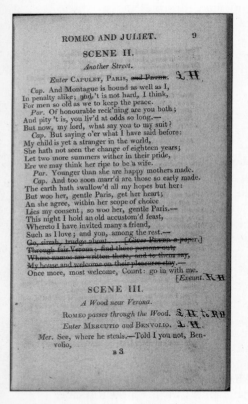

Act 1, Scene 2 in J. P. Kemble's production is very short. The lines where Capulet asks Peter to find the guests are cut; thus, the encounter between Peter and Romeo and his friends is also eliminated.

ROMEO
  Whither? To supper?

Servant
  To our house.

ROMEO
  Whose house?

Servant
  My master's.   75

ROMEO
  Indeed, I should have asked you that before.

Servant
  Now I'll tell you without asking. My master is the great rich Capulet,
  and if you be not of the house of Montagues, I pray, come and crush a
  cup of wine. Rest you merry.

                                                                  [*Exit*]

BENVOLIO
  At this same ancient feast of Capulet's   80
  Sups the fair Rosaline whom thou so loves
  With all the admired beauties of Verona.
  Go thither and with unattainted eye,
  Compare her face with some that I shall show,
  And I will make thee think thy swan a crow.   85

ROMEO
  When the devout religion of mine eye
  Maintains such falsehood, then turn tears to fires,
  And these, who often drowned could never die,
  Transparent heretics be burnt for liars.
  One fairer than my love the all-seeing sun   90
  Ne'er saw her match since first the world begun.

BENVOLIO
  Tut, you saw her fair, none else being by,
  Herself poised with herself in either eye,

94: **that crystal scales:** Benvolio is referring to Romeo's eyes

97: **scant:** scarcely, hardly

But in that crystal scales, let there be weighed
Your lady's love against some other maid   95
That I will show you shining at this feast,
And she shall scant show well that now seems best.

ROMEO
I'll go along, no such sight to be shown,
But to rejoice in splendor of mine own.

[Exeunt]

Scenes 2 and 3 in the 1936 Cukor movie production are set in and around the Capulet courtyard.

Courtesy: Douglas Lanier

1–68:
Fiona Shaw as the Nurse, Frances Barber as Lady Capulet
Dame Flora Robson as the Nurse, Rachel Kempson as Lady Capulet

2: **maidenhead:** virginity

14: **She's not fourteen:** In the 1811 Garrick-Kemble production, Juliet's age is advanced from fourteen to nearly eighteen, partly perhaps so that older actresses like Sarah Siddons would not look too out-of-place in the part.

Act 1: Scene 3]

[*Enter LADY CAPULET and NURSE*]

LADY CAPULET
Nurse, where's my daughter? Call her forth to me.

NURSE
Now, by my maidenhead, at twelve year old,
I bade her come. What, lamb! What, ladybird!
God forbid! Where's this girl? What, Juliet!

[*Enter JULIET*]

JULIET
How now, who calls?   5

NURSE
                    Your mother.

JULIET
                              Madam, I am here.
What is your will?

LADY CAPULET
This is the matter. — Nurse, give leave awhile,
We must talk in secret. — Nurse, come back again;   10
I have remembered me; thou's hear our counsel.
Thou knowest my daughter's of a pretty age.

NURSE
Faith, I can tell her age unto an hour.

LADY CAPULET
She's not fourteen.

tracks 1-2

1–68:
Fiona Shaw as the Nurse, Frances Barber as Lady Capulet
Dame Flora Robson as the Nurse, Rachel Kempson as Lady Capulet

18: **Lammastide:** the first of August, a Christian feasting day based on a similar pagan harvest holiday

21: **Lammas Eve:** day before Lammastide, July 31

26: **marry:** exclamation meaning "indeed"

30: **wormwood:** a plant that yields a bitter dark green oil used in absinthe; proverbial for bitterness (presumably used to wean Juliet from being breastfed)

30: **dug:** breast

36: **tetchy:** fretful, peevish

37: **"Shake" quoth the dove-house:** The dove-house shook (from the child's crying)

37: **I trow:** I dare say

38: **trudge:** to trot, to run hastily and heavily

40: **rood:** the holy cross, crucifix

42: **broke her brow:** scraped her head

47: **holidame:** sanctity, salvation; used in swearing

NURSE
> I'll lay fourteen of my teeth, —   15
And yet, to my teen be it spoken, I have but four —
She's not fourteen. How long is it now
To Lammastide?

LADY CAPULET
> A fortnight and odd days.

NURSE
Even or odd, of all days in the year,   20
Come Lammas Eve at night shall she be fourteen.
Susan and she — God rest all Christian souls! —
Were of an age. Well, Susan is with God;
She was too good for me. But, as I said,
On Lammas Eve at night shall she be fourteen.   25
That shall she; marry, I remember it well.
'Tis since the earthquake now eleven years;
And she was weaned, — I never shall forget it, —
Of all the days of the year, upon that day,
For I had then laid wormwood to my dug,   30
Sitting in the sun under the dove-house wall.
My lord and you were then at Mantua; —
Nay, I do bear a brain. But, as I said,
When it did taste the wormwood on the nipple
Of my dug and felt it bitter, pretty fool,   35
To see it tetchy and fall out with the dug.
"Shake," quoth the dove-house. 'Twas no need, I trow,
To bid me trudge.
And since that time it is eleven years,
For then she could stand alone; nay, by the rood,   40
She could have run and waddled all about.
For even the day before, she broke her brow,
And then my husband — God be with his soul!
He was a merry man — took up the child.
"Yea," quoth he, "dost thou fall upon thy face?   45
Thou wilt fall backward when thou hast more wit,
Wilt thou not, Jule?" And, by my holidame,
The pretty wretch left crying and said "Ay."

1–68:
Fiona Shaw as the Nurse, Frances Barber as Lady Capulet
Dame Flora Robson as the Nurse, Rachel Kempson as Lady Capulet

52: **stinted:** stopped (crying)

58: **parlous knock:** alarming blow (parlous = popular corruption of *perilous* meaning alarming)

Line 64: "Thou wast the prettiest babe that e'er I nursed": Marin Hinkle as Juliet and Jean Stapleton as the Nurse in The Shakespeare Theatre's 1993–1994 production directed by Barry Kyle
Photo: Richard Anderson

To see, now, how a jest shall come about!
I warrant, an I should live a thousand years,   50
I never should forget it. "Wilt thou not, Jule?" quoth he.
And, pretty fool, it stinted and said "Ay."

LADY CAPULET
Enough of this; I pray thee, hold thy peace.

NURSE
Yes, madam, yet I cannot choose but laugh,
To think it should leave crying and say "Ay."   55
And yet, I warrant, it had upon its brow
A bump as big as a young cockerel's stone,
A parlous knock, and it cried bitterly.
"Yea," quoth my husband, "fallest upon thy face?
Thou wilt fall backward when thou comest to age,   60
Wilt thou not, Jule?" It stinted and said "Ay."

JULIET
And stint thou too, I pray thee, nurse, say I.

NURSE
Peace, I have done. God mark thee to his grace.
Thou wast the prettiest babe that e'er I nursed,
An I might live to see thee married once,   65
I have my wish.

LADY CAPULET
Marry, that "marry" is the very theme
I came to talk of. Tell me, daughter Juliet,
How stands your disposition to be married?

JULIET
It is an honour that I dream not of.   70

NURSE
An honour? Were not I thine only nurse,
I would say thou hadst sucked wisdom from thy
        teat.

80: **he's a man of wax:** he's as pretty as if he had been modelled in wax

87: **married lineament:** harmonious feature

90: **margent:** Glosses or comments, in old books, usually printed on the margin

LADY CAPULET
    Well, think of marriage now. Younger than you,
    Here in Verona, ladies of esteem
    Are made already mothers. By my count,   75
    I was your mother much upon these years
    That you are now a maid. Thus, then, in brief,
    The valiant Paris seeks you for his love.

NURSE
    A man, young lady — lady, such a man
    As all the world — why, he's a man of wax.   80

LADY CAPULET
    Verona's summer hath not such a flower.

NURSE
    Nay, he's a flower; in faith, a very flower.

LADY CAPULET
    What say you? Can you love the gentleman?
    This night you shall behold him at our feast;
    Read o'er the volume of young Paris' face,   85
    And find delight writ there with beauty's pen.
    Examine every married lineament,
    And see how one another lends content,
    And what obscured in this fair volume lies
    Find written in the margent of his eyes.   90
    This precious book of love, this unbound lover,
    To beautify him only lacks a cover.
    The fish lives in the sea, and 'tis much pride
    For fair without the fair within to hide.
    That book in many's eyes doth share the glory   95
    That in gold clasps locks in the golden story.
    So shall you share all that he doth possess
    By having him, making yourself no less.

NURSE
    No less? Nay, bigger. Women grow by men.

101: **I'll look...liking move:** i.e., I'll look and see if I find him attractive

102: **endart:** to let fly and pierce like an arrow

106: **in extremity:** to the highest degree is in an uproar

108: **stays:** waits

Line 109: "Go, girl, seek happy nights to happy days": Cynthia Nixon as Juliet and Anne Meara as the Nurse in the Public Theater's 1987–88 production directed by Les Waters

Photo: George E. Joseph

LADY CAPULET

Speak briefly, can you like of Paris' love?   100

JULIET

I'll look to like, if looking liking move,
But no more deep will I endart mine eye
Than your consent gives strength to make it fly.

[Enter Servingman]

Servant

Madam, the guests are come, supper served up, you called, my
young lady asked for, the nurse cursed in the pantry, and everything   105
in extremity. I must hence to wait; I beseech you, follow straight.

LADY CAPULET

We follow thee.

[Exit Servingman]

Juliet, the County stays.

NURSE

Go, girl, seek happy nights to happy days.

[Exeunt]

Ian McKellen as Romeo and Michael Pennington as Mercutio on their way to the Capulet feast

Royal Shakespeare Company (1976)

Stage direction: **Maskers:** participants in a costume party

3: **The date is out of such prolixity:** i.e., Such wordiness (prolixity) is outdated (the date is out)

4: **hoodwinked:** blindfolded

5: **bow of lath:** cheap wooden bow

6: **crow-keeper:** scarecrow

7: **without-book:** recited by heart

9: **measure:** judge

10: **measure:** mete out, provide

10: **measure:** a dance

12: **heavy:** sad, with a pun on light

18: **bound:** limit

Act 1: Scene 4]

[*Enter ROMEO, MERCUTIO, BENVOLIO,*
with five or six other Maskers, Torchbearers]

ROMEO
    What, shall this speech be spoke for our excuse?
    Or shall we on without apology?

BENVOLIO
    The date is out of such prolixity.
    We'll have no Cupid hoodwinked with a scarf,
    Bearing a Tartar's painted bow of lath,   5
    Scaring the ladies like a crow-keeper,
    Nor no without-book prologue, faintly spoke
    After the prompter, for our entrance.
    But let them measure us by what they will;
    We'll measure them a measure and be gone.   10

ROMEO
    Give me a torch. I am not for this ambling;
    Being but heavy, I will bear the light.

MERCUTIO
    Nay, gentle Romeo, we must have you dance.

ROMEO
    Not I, believe me. You have dancing shoes
    With nimble soles; I have a soul of lead   15
    So stakes me to the ground I cannot move.

MERCUTIO
    You are a lover; borrow Cupid's wings,
    And soar with them above a common bound.

20: **bound:** restricted

21: **bound:** leap

21: **pitch:** height

30: **a visor for a visor:** a mask for his face (which itself is like a mask)

32: **beetle brows:** prominent eyebrows

36: **rushes:** a kind of plant used as floor coverings

37: **grandsire phrase:** old saying

38: **candle-holder:** he who holds the candle and is an assistant, but not a partaker, of the pleasure of others

40: **dun's the mouse:** a proverbial saying without any distinct meaning, perhaps used as a pun on Romeo's "done"

42: **save your reverence:** an old formula of apology for introducing an indelicate expression

ROMEO

 I am too sore enpierced with his shaft
 To soar with his light feathers, and so bound,   20
 I cannot bound a pitch above dull woe.
 Under love's heavy burden do I sink.

MERCUTIO

 And to sink in it should you burden love —
 Too great oppression for a tender thing.

ROMEO

 Is love a tender thing? It is too rough,   25
 Too rude, too boisterous, and it pricks like thorn.

MERCUTIO

 If love be rough with you, be rough with love.
 Prick love for pricking, and you beat love down. —
 Give me a case to put my visage in. —
 A visor for a visor; what care I   30
 What curious eye doth quote deformities?
 Here are the beetle brows shall blush for me.

BENVOLIO

 Come, knock and enter, and no sooner in,
 But every man betake him to his legs.

ROMEO

 A torch for me. Let wantons light of heart   35
 Tickle the senseless rushes with their heels,
 For I am proverbed with a grandsire phrase.
 I'll be a candle-holder and look on.
 The game was ne'er so fair, and I am done.

MERCUTIO

 Tut, dun's the mouse, the constable's own word.   40
 If thou art dun, we'll draw thee from the mire
 Of, save your reverence, love, wherein thou stickest
 Up to the ears. Come, we burn daylight, ho!

57: **Queen Mab:** the queen of the fairies

tracks 3-4

57–109:
Anton Lesser as Mercutio, Michael Sheen as Romeo
Ian Bannen as Mercutio, Keith Michell as Romeo

Line 57: "O, then I see Queen Mab hath been with you": Roy Scheider as Mercutio
in the 1961 production by the Public Theater directed by Joseph Papp
Photo: George E. Joseph

59: **agate stone:** stone of the flint kind, often worn in rings, with little figures
cut in it

60: **alderman:** member of a city corporation

61: **atomies:** atoms (indicates the very diminutive steeds that draw Queen Mab's
chariot)

ROMEO
   Nay, that's not so.

MERCUTIO
                  I mean, sir, in delay   45
   We waste our lights in vain, light lights by day.
   Take our good meaning, for our judgment sits
   Five times in that, ere once in our five wits.

ROMEO
   And we mean well in going to this masque,
   But 'tis no wit to go.   50

MERCUTIO
                  Why, may one ask?

ROMEO
   I dreamt a dream tonight.

MERCUTIO
                  And so did I.

ROMEO
   Well, what was yours?

MERCUTIO
                  That dreamers often lie.   55

ROMEO
   In bed asleep, while they do dream things true.

MERCUTIO
   O, then I see Queen Mab hath been with you.
   She is the fairies' midwife, and she comes
   In shape no bigger than an agate stone
   On the forefinger of an alderman,   60
   Drawn with a team of little atomies
   Over men's noses as they lie asleep.
   Her wagon spokes made of long spinners' legs,

tracks 3-4

57–109:
Anton Lesser as Mercutio, Michael Sheen as Romeo
Ian Bannen as Mercutio, Keith Michell as Romeo

68: **waggoner:** charioteer

72: **joiner:** maker of wooden furniture

80: **sweetmeats:** fruits preserved with sugar, especially perfumed sugar-plums

82: **smelling out a suit:** looking for bribes or payments from court petitioners (suit = favor from the court)

83: **tithe-pig:** pig given to the church as tithe

85: **benefice:** an ecclesiastical living

88: **ambuscadoes:** Spanish blades

89: **healths:** (drinking) toasts

93: **plats:** braids

94: **elf-locks in foul sluttish hairs:** locks so tangled they were supposed to be the operation of fairies

The cover, of the wings of grasshoppers,
Her traces, of the smallest spider's web,   65
Her collars, of the moonshine's watery beams,
Her whip, of cricket's bone, the lash of film,
Her waggoner, a small grey-coated gnat,
Not half so big as a round little worm
Pricked from the lazy finger of a maid.   70
Her chariot is an empty hazel-nut
Made by the joiner squirrel or old grub,
Time out o' mind the fairies' coachmakers.
And in this state she gallops night by night
Through lovers' brains, and then they dream of love;   75
On courtiers' knees, that dream on curtsies straight;
O'er lawyers' fingers, who straight dream on fees;
O'er ladies' lips, who straight on kisses dream,
Which oft the angry Mab with blisters plagues
Because their breaths with sweetmeats tainted are.   80
Sometime she gallops o'er a courtier's nose,
And then dreams he of smelling out a suit;
And sometime comes she with a tithe-pig's tail
Tickling a parson's nose as he lies asleep,
Then he dreams of another benefice.   85
Sometime she driveth o'er a soldier's neck,
And then dreams he of cutting foreign throats,
Of breaches, ambuscadoes, Spanish blades,
Of healths five fathom deep; and then anon
Drums in his ear, at which he starts and wakes,   90
And being thus frighted, swears a prayer or two
And sleeps again. This is that very Mab
That plats the manes of horses in the night
And bakes the elf-locks in foul sluttish hairs
Which, once untangled, much misfortune bodes.   95
This is the hag, when maids lie on their backs,
That presses them and learns them first to bear,
Making them women of good carriage.
This is she —

ROMEO
                    Peace, peace, Mercutio, peace.   100
Thou talk'st of nothing.

tracks 3-4

57–109:
Anton Lesser as Mercutio, Michael Sheen as Romeo
Ian Bannen as Mercutio, Keith Michell as Romeo

Line 102: "True, I talk of dreams": Robert Petkoff as Mercutio with Ensemble in Chicago Shakespeare Theater's 2005 production, directed by Mark Lamos
Photo: Liz Lauren

109: **dew-dropping:** rainy

112: **misgives:** has a presentiment of evil

MERCUTIO
                    True, I talk of dreams,
    Which are the children of an idle brain,
    Begot of nothing but vain fantasy,
    Which is as thin of substance as the air   105
    And more inconstant than the wind, who woos
    Even now the frozen bosom of the north,
    And, being angered, puffs away from thence,
    Turning his side to the dew-dropping south.

BENVOLIO
    This wind you talk of blows us from ourselves.   110
    Supper is done, and we shall come too late.

ROMEO
    I fear too early, for my mind misgives
    Some consequence, yet hanging in the stars,
    Shall bitterly begin his fearful date
    With this night's revels and expire the term   115
    Of a despisèd life closed in my breast
    By some vile forfeit of untimely death.
    But he that hath the steerage of my course
    Direct my suit. On, lusty gentlemen.

BENVOLIO
    Strike, drum.   120
                            [*They march about the stage*]

1: trencher: a large serving plate, often ceremonial

5: joint-stools: a folding-chair

5: court-cupboard: a moveable buffet or closet, in which plate and other articles of luxury were displayed

6: marchpane: a sweet biscuit composed of sugar and almonds (marzipan)

16: makes dainty: gives oneself airs, behaves primly

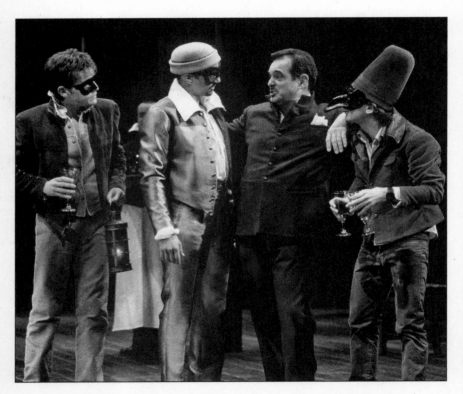

Line 18: "Welcome, gentlemen!": The ensemble of The Shakespeare Theatre's 1993–1994 production directed by Barry Kyle

Photo: Richard Anderson

Act 1: Scene 5

[Enter Servingmen with napkins]

First Servingman
Where's Potpan that he helps not to take away? He shift a trencher?
He scrape a trencher?

Second Servingman
When good manners shall lie all in one or two men's hands and they
unwashed too, 'tis a foul thing.

First Servingman
Away with the joint-stools, remove the court-cupboard, look to the plate.   5
Good thou, save me a piece of marchpane, and as thou loves me, let the
porter let in Susan Grindstone and Nell. — Anthony and Potpan!

Third Servingman
Ay, boy, ready.

First Servingman
You are looked for and called for, asked for and sought for in the great
chamber.   10

Third Servingman
We cannot be here and there too. — Cheerly, boys. Be brisk awhile,
and the longer liver take all.
               [Enter all the guests and gentlewomen to the Maskers]

CAPULET
Welcome, gentlemen! Ladies that have their toes
Unplagued with corns will walk a bout with you. —
Ah, my mistresses, which of you all   15
Will now deny to dance? She that makes dainty,
She, I'll swear, hath corns. Am I come near ye now? —
Welcome, gentlemen! I have seen the day

23: **A hall, a hall:** a cry to make room in a crowd

26: **unlooked-for:** unexpected

34: **Pentecost:** a Christian feast on the seventh Sunday after Easter

39: **ward:** one under the care of a guardian; a minor

Lines 40–41: "What lady's that, which doth enrich the hand / Of yonder knight?":
Norma Shearer as Juliet, Ralph Forbes as Paris, and ensemble in George Cukor's
1936 movie production
Courtesy: Douglas Lanier

That I have worn a visor and could tell
A whispering tale in a fair lady's ear,   20
Such as would please. 'Tis gone, 'tis gone, 'tis gone.
You are welcome, gentlemen! — Come, musicians, play.
                         [*Music plays, and they dance*]
A hall, a hall! Give room! — And foot it, girls. —
More light, you knaves, and turn the tables up,
And quench the fire; the room is grown too hot.   25
Ah, sirrah, this unlooked-for sport comes well. —
Nay, sit, nay, sit, good cousin Capulet,
For you and I are past our dancing days.
How long is't now since last yourself and I
Were in a mask?   30

Second Capulet
                    By'r lady, thirty years.

CAPULET
What, man! 'Tis not so much, 'tis not so much.
'Tis since the nuptials of Lucentio,
Come Pentecost as quickly as it will,
Some five and twenty years, and then we masked.   35

Second Capulet
'Tis more, 'tis more, his son is elder, sir;
His son is thirty.

CAPULET
                    Will you tell me that?
His son was but a ward two years ago.

ROMEO
                                        [*To a Servingman*]
What lady's that which doth enrich the hand   40
Of yonder knight?

Servant
I know not, sir.

55: **antic face:** odd or fantastic mask

56: **fleer:** smile or grin contemptuously

66: **portly:** dignified

ROMEO

O, she doth teach the torches to burn bright.
It seems she hangs upon the cheek of night
As a rich jewel in an Ethiope's ear;   45
Beauty too rich for use, for earth too dear.
So shows a snowy dove trooping with crows,
As yonder lady o'er her fellows shows.
The measure done, I'll watch her place of stand,
And, touching hers, make blessèd my rude hand.   50
Did my heart love till now? Forswear it, sight,
For I ne'er saw true beauty till this night.

TYBALT

This, by his voice, should be a Montague. —
Fetch me my rapier, boy. — What dares the slave
Come hither, covered with an antic face,   55
To fleer and scorn at our solemnity?
Now, by the stock and honour of my kin,
To strike him dead, I hold it not a sin.

CAPULET

Why, how now, kinsman. Wherefore storm you so?

TYBALT

Uncle, this is a Montague, our foe,   60
A villain that is hither come in spite,
To scorn at our solemnity this night.

CAPULET

Young Romeo is it?

TYBALT

                        'Tis he, that villain, Romeo.

CAPULET

Content thee, gentle coz, let him alone.   65
He bears him like a portly gentleman,
And, to say truth, Verona brags of him
To be a virtuous and well-governed youth.

74: **ill-beseeming semblance:** unbecoming appearance

78: **goodman:** title under the rank of gentleman (here used disparagingly)

82: **You will set cock-a-hoop:** you will pick a quarrel; you will play the bully

87: **contrary:** oppose, cross

88: **princox:** an impertinent child, a rascal

91: **Patience perforce:** enforced and constrained calm

91: **wilful choler:** ready anger

I would not for the wealth of all the town
Here in my house do him disparagement.   70
Therefore be patient, take no note of him.
It is my will, the which if thou respect,
Show a fair presence and put off these frowns,
An ill-beseeming semblance for a feast.

TYBALT
It fits, when such a villain is a guest.   75
I'll not endure him.

CAPULET
    He shall be endured.
What, goodman boy? I say, he shall. Go to.
Am I the master here or you? Go to.
You'll not endure him. God shall mend my soul.   80
You'll make a mutiny among my guests.
You will set cock-a-hoop; you'll be the man.

TYBALT
Why, uncle, 'tis a shame.

CAPULET
    Go to, go to.
You are a saucy boy. Is't so, indeed?   85
This trick may chance to scathe you. I know what;
You must contrary me. Marry, 'tis time. —
Well said, my hearts! — You are a princox; go. —
Be quiet, or — More light, more light! For shame!
I'll make you quiet. — What, cheerly, my hearts!   90

TYBALT
Patience perforce with wilful choler meeting
Makes my flesh tremble in their different greeting.
I will withdraw, but this intrusion shall
Now seeming sweet convert to bitt'rest gall.

                [Exit]

95–108: **If I profane...effect I take:** Modern editors observe that these 14 lines are structured as a sonnet.

tracks 5–6

95–112:
Estelle Kohler as Juliet, Bill Homewood as Romeo
Kate Beckinsale as Juliet, Michael Sheen as Romeo

Line 98: "To smooth that rough touch with a tender kiss": Claire Danes as Juliet and Leonardo DiCaprio as Romeo in *William Shakespeare's Romeo + Juliet*, directed by Baz Luhrmann
Courtesy: 20th Century Fox

102: **palmers:** pilgrims (properly ones from the Holy Land, bearing palm-leaves)

113: **by th' book:** according to prescription, with due formality

ROMEO

[*To JULIET*]
95

If I profane with my unworthiest hand
This holy shrine, the gentle fine is this.
My lips, two blushing pilgrims, ready stand
To smooth that rough touch with a tender kiss.

JULIET

Good pilgrim, you do wrong your hand too much,
Which mannerly devotion shows in this,   100
For saints have hands that pilgrims' hands do touch,
And palm to palm is holy palmers' kiss.

ROMEO

Have not saints lips and holy palmers too?

JULIET

Ay, pilgrim, lips that they must use in prayer.

ROMEO

O, then, dear saint, let lips do what hands do.   105
They pray, grant thou, lest faith turn to despair.

JULIET

Saints do not move, though grant for prayers' sake.

ROMEO

Then move not while my prayer's effect I take.
Thus from my lips, by thine, my sin is purged.

JULIET

Then have my lips the sin that they have took.   110

ROMEO

Sin from my lips? O trespass sweetly urged!
Give me my sin again.

JULIET

You kiss by th' book.

119: **withal:** with

121: **chinks:** slang for money

127: **towards:** in preparation, at hand

131: **fay:** faith

NURSE
  Madam, your mother craves a word with you.

ROMEO
  What is her mother?   115

NURSE
                    Marry, bachelor,
  Her mother is the lady of the house,
  And a good lady, and a wise and virtuous.
  I nursed her daughter, that you talked withal.
  I tell you, he that can lay hold of her   120
  Shall have the chinks.

ROMEO
                    Is she a Capulet?
  O dear account! My life is my foe's debt.

BENVOLIO
  Away, begone; the sport is at the best.

ROMEO
  Ay, so I fear; the more is my unrest.   125

CAPULET
  Nay, gentlemen, prepare not to be gone.
  We have a trifling foolish banquet towards.
  Is it e'en so? Why, then, I thank you all.
  I thank you, honest gentlemen. Good night. —
  More torches here! — Come on then, let's to bed. —   130
  Ah, sirrah, by my fay, it waxes late.
  I'll to my rest.

                              [*Exeunt all but JULIET and NURSE*]

JULIET
  Come hither, Nurse. What is yond gentleman?

NURSE
  The son and heir of old Tiberio.

143–146: **My only love...a loathèd enemy:** The novelty of this revelation is a little puzzling in this Garrick-Kemble version, since Romeo has worshipped Juliet for quite some time now, but this is Garrick's way of getting rid of Rosaline. Garrick is determined that Romeo be in love with Juliet from the start and with no one else.

145: **prodigious:** ominous, portentous

JULIET
  What's he that now is going out of door?   135

NURSE
  Marry, that, I think, be young Petruchio.

JULIET
  What's he that follows here, that would not dance?

NURSE
  I know not.

JULIET
  Go ask his name. If he be married,
  My grave is like to be my wedding bed.   140

NURSE
  His name is Romeo, and a Montague,
  The only son of your great enemy.

JULIET
  My only love sprung from my only hate!
  Too early seen unknown, and known too late!
  Prodigious birth of love it is to me,   145
  That I must love a loathèd enemy.

NURSE
  What's this? What's this?

JULIET
                  A rhyme I learned even now
  Of one I danced withal.

                                      [*One calls within "Juliet."*]

NURSE
                  Anon, anon!   150
  Come, let's away; the strangers all are gone.

                                                          [*Exeunt*]

[Romeo and Juliet

Act 2

2: **gapes:** greedily longs for

3: **That fair:** i.e., Rosaline

7: **complain:** lament

14: **Tempering...sweet:** countering great difficulties (extremities) with great delights (extreme sweet)

CHORUS
　Now old desire doth in his deathbed lie,
　And young affection gapes to be his heir,
　That fair for which love groaned for and would die,
　With tender Juliet matched is now not fair.
　Now Romeo is beloved and loves again,　　　　　　　5
　Alike betwitched by the charm of looks,
　But to his foe supposed he must complain,
　And she steal love's sweet bait from fearful hooks.
　Being held a foe, he may not have access
　To breathe such vows as lovers use to swear;　　　10
　And she as much in love, her means much less
　To meet her new beloved anywhere.
　But passion lends them power, time means, to meet,
　Tempering extremities with extreme sweet.

[*Exit*]

Scene: In the Garrick-Kemble text this scene is labeled as taking place in *An Open Place, adjoining Capulet's Garden.* Once Mercutio and Benvolio go off, having concluded that Romeo is nowhere to be found, we are introduced to a new scene: *Capulet's Garden.* A stage direction specifies that Juliet *"appears at a Balcony, and sits down."* (See page 16.)

Set rendering of Capulet's Garden and Balcony from the New Theatre's 1935 production directed by Sir John Gielgud

Rare Book and Special Collections Library, University of Illinois at Urbana-Champaign

9: **humours:** passions

14: **purblind:** quite blind (a reference to blindfolded Cupid)

15: **Abraham:** reference to the biblical old man

15: **trim:** true, on the mark

16: **King Cophetua loved the beggar-maid:** reference to an Old English ballad

18: **ape:** term of endearment, used here for Romeo

Act 2: Scene 1]

[Enter ROMEO]

ROMEO
  Can I go forward when my heart is here?
  Turn back, dull earth, and find thy centre out.

[ROMEO hides]
[Enter BENVOLIO and MERCUTIO]

BENVOLIO
  Romeo! My cousin Romeo! Romeo!

MERCUTIO
  He is wise,
  And, on my life, hath stol'n him home to bed.   5

BENVOLIO
  He ran this way, and leapt this orchard wall.
  Call, good Mercutio.

MERCUTIO
                    Nay, I'll conjure too.
  Romeo! Humours! Madman! Passion! Lover!
  Appear thou in the likeness of a sigh.   10
  Speak but one rhyme, and I am satisfied.
  Cry but "Ay me," pronounce but "love" and "dove."
  Speak to my gossip Venus one fair word,
  One nickname for her purblind son and heir,
  Young Abraham Cupid, he that shot so trim,   15
  When King Cophetua loved the beggar-maid. —
  He heareth not, he stirreth not, he moveth not.
  The ape is dead, and I must conjure him. —
  I conjure thee by Rosaline's bright eyes,
  By her high forehead and her scarlet lip,   20
  By her fine foot, straight leg, and quivering thigh,

22: **demesnes:** district, territory

33: **consorted:** associated, accompanied

33: **humorous:** damp, heavy (also in an emotional sense)

38: **medlars:** small, applelike fruits; also slang for the female sex organ

40: **open-arse:** describing the medlar, but also being sexually explicit

40: **pop'rin pear:** pear named for *Poperingue*, a town in Flanders; also slang for the male sex organ

41: **truckle-bed:** trundle bed, a bed that runs on wheels and may be pushed under another. Trundle beds were mostly used by lower classes, so Mercutio is being overly modest for humorous purposes.

And the demesnes that there adjacent lie,
That in thy likeness thou appear to us!

BENVOLIO
And if he hear thee, thou wilt anger him.

MERCUTIO
This cannot anger him. 'Twould anger him   25
To raise a spirit in his mistress' circle
Of some strange nature, letting it there stand
Till she had laid it and conjured it down.
That were some spite. My invocation
Is fair and honest. In his mistress' name   30
I conjure only but to raise up him.

BENVOLIO
Come, he hath hid himself among these trees,
To be consorted with the humorous night.
Blind is his love and best befits the dark.

MERCUTIO
If love be blind, love cannot hit the mark.   35
Now will he sit under a medlar tree,
And wish his mistress were that kind of fruit
As maids call medlars, when they laugh alone.
O, Romeo, that she were, O, that she were
An open-arse, or thou a pop'rin pear!   40
Romeo, good night. I'll to my truckle-bed;
This field-bed is too cold for me to sleep. —
Come, shall we go?

BENVOLIO
                Go, then, for 'tis in vain
To seek him here that means not to be found.   45
                                              [*Exeunt*]

Scene: **JULIET appears above:** Shakespeare never uses the word "balcony" in this or any other play. The "balcony" was inherited by Garrick and Kemble from performance traditions of the Restoration and early eighteenth century; a balcony suited well the staging methods of the era and turns up regularly in graphic illustrations of the scene.

2–34:
Joseph Fiennes as Romeo, Maria Miles as Juliet
Albert Finney as Romeo, Claire Bloom as Juliet

8: **vestal livery:** costume worn by maidens of Diana, the Roman goddess of chastity, hunting, and the moon

8: **sick and green:** referring to greensickness, a kind of anemia called chlorosis, affecting young women

SCENE II.

Capulet's Garden.

Enter ROMEO. R. H. S. E.

Rom. He jests at scars that never felt a wound.
　　　[JULIET *appears at a Balcony, and sits down.*]
But, soft! What light thro' yonder window breaks!
It is the east, and Juliet is the sun!
Arise, fair sun, and kill the envious moon,
Who is already sick and pale with grief,
That thou, her maid, art far more fair than she.—
She speaks, yet she says nothing: What of that?
Her eye discourses: I will answer it.—
I am too bold.—O, were those eyes in heaven,
They would through the airy region stream so bright,
That birds would sing, and think it were the morn.—

The stage direction in J. P. Kemble's production

Act 2: Scene 2]

ROMEO
    He jests at scars that never felt a wound.

    But, soft! What light through yonder window breaks?
    It is the east, and Juliet is the sun.
    Arise, fair sun, and kill the envious moon
    Who is already sick and pale with grief   5
    That thou her maid art far more fair than she.
    Be not her maid, since she is envious;
    Her vestal livery is but sick and green
    And none but fools do wear it. Cast it off.
    It is my lady, O, it is my love!   10
    O, that she knew she were!
    She speaks, yet she says nothing. What of that?
    Her eye discourses; I will answer it.
    I am too bold, 'tis not to me she speaks.
    Two of the fairest stars in all the heaven,   15
    Having some business, do entreat her eyes
    To twinkle in their spheres till they return.
    What if her eyes were there, they in her head?
    The brightness of her cheek would shame those stars
    As daylight doth a lamp. Her eyes in heaven   20
    Would through the airy region stream so bright
    That birds would sing and think it were not night.
    See how she leans her cheek upon her hand.
    O, that I were a glove upon that hand,
    That I might touch that cheek!   25

JULIET
          Ay me.

tracks 7-8

2–34:
Joseph Fiennes as Romeo, Maria Miles as Juliet
Albert Finney as Romeo, Claire Bloom as Juliet

Jennifer Ikeda as Juliet and Paul Whitthorne as Romeo in The Shakespeare Theatre's 2001–2002 production directed by Rachel Kavanaugh
Photo: Carol Rosegg

35: **wherefore:** why

tracks 9-10

35–85:
Maria Miles as Juliet, Joseph Fiennes as Romeo
Claire Bloom as Juliet, Albert Finney as Romeo

37: **wilt:** will

41: **though not a Montague:** even without the name Montague

48: **owes:** owns

ROMEO
     She speaks!
O, speak again, bright angel, for thou art
As glorious to this night, being o'er my head,
As is a wingèd messenger of heaven   30
Unto the white-upturned, wond'ring eyes
Of mortals that fall back to gaze on him
When he bestrides the lazy puffing clouds
And sails upon the bosom of the air.

JULIET
O Romeo, Romeo, wherefore art thou Romeo?   35
Deny thy father and refuse thy name,
Or, if thou wilt not, be but sworn my love,
And I'll no longer be a Capulet.

ROMEO
[*Aside*] Shall I hear more, or shall I speak at this?

JULIET
'Tis but thy name that is my enemy.   40
Thou art thyself, though not a Montague.
What's Montague? It is nor hand, nor foot,
Nor arm, nor face, nor any other part
Belonging to a man. O, be some other name!
What's in a name? That which we call a rose   45
By any other word would smell as sweet;
So Romeo would, were he not Romeo called.
Retain that dear perfection which he owes
Without that title. Romeo, doff thy name,
And for thy name which is no part of thee,   50
Take all myself.

ROMEO
     I take thee at thy word.
Call me but love, and I'll be new baptized.
Henceforth, I never will be Romeo.

tracks 9-10

35–85:
Maria Miles as Juliet, Joseph Fiennes as Romeo
Claire Bloom as Juliet, Albert Finney as Romeo

70: **o'er-perch:** fly over

71: **stony limits:** i.e., the walls

77: **proof against:** safe from, protected from

JULIET

    What man art thou that thus bescreened in night   55
    So stumblest on my counsel?

ROMEO

                By a name
    I know not how to tell thee who I am.
    My name, dear saint, is hateful to myself
    Because it is an enemy to thee;   60
    Had I it written, I would tear the word.

JULIET

    My ears have yet not drunk a hundred words
    Of thy tongue's uttering, yet I know the sound.
    Art thou not Romeo and a Montague?

ROMEO

    Neither, fair maid, if either thee dislike.   65

JULIET

    How camest thou hither, tell me, and wherefore?
    The orchard walls are high and hard to climb,
    And the place death, considering who thou art,
    If any of my kinsmen find thee here.

ROMEO

    With love's light wings did I o'er-perch these walls,   70
    For stony limits cannot hold love out,
    And what love can do that dares love attempt;
    Therefore, thy kinsmen are no stop to me.

JULIET

    If they do see thee, they will murder thee.

ROMEO

    Alack, there lies more peril in thine eye   75
    Than twenty of their swords. Look thou but sweet,
    And I am proof against their enmity.

tracks 9-10

35–85:
Maria Miles as Juliet, Joseph Fiennes as Romeo
Claire Bloom as Juliet, Albert Finney as Romeo

82: **proroguèd:** delayed

92: **fain:** gladly, willingly

97: **Jove:** Jupiter, the supreme god of the Romans

103: **'havior light:** full of levity, frivolous

105: **strange:** reserved, distant

107: **ware:** aware

JULIET
   I would not for the world they saw thee here.

ROMEO
   I have night's cloak to hide me from their eyes,
   And but thou love me, let them find me here.   80
   My life were better ended by their hate,
   Than death proroguèd, wanting of thy love.

JULIET
   By whose direction found'st thou out this place?

ROMEO
   By love, that first did prompt me to inquire.
   He lent me counsel, and I lent him eyes.   85
   I am no pilot; yet, wert thou as far
   As that vast shore washed with the farthest sea,
   I should adventure for such merchandise.

JULIET
   Thou knowest the mask of night is on my face,
   Else would a maiden blush bepaint my cheek,   90
   For that which thou hast heard me speak to-night.
   Fain would I dwell on form, fain, fain deny
   What I have spoke, but farewell compliment.
   Dost thou love me? I know thou wilt say "Ay,"
   And I will take thy word. Yet if thou swear'st,   95
   Thou mayst prove false. At lovers' perjuries,
   They say, Jove laughs. O gentle Romeo,
   If thou dost love, pronounce it faithfully,
   Or if thou think'st I am too quickly won,
   I'll frown and be perverse and say thee nay,   100
   So thou wilt woo, but else, not for the world.
   In truth, fair Montague, I am too fond,
   And therefore thou mayst think my 'havior light.
   But trust me, gentleman, I'll prove more true
   Than those that have more coying to be strange.   105
   I should have been more strange, I must confess,
   But that thou overheard'st, ere I was ware

113: **inconstant:** fickle, unreliable

Line 113: "O, swear not by the moon, th' inconstant moon": Leslie Howard as Romeo and Norma Shearer as Juliet in George Cukor's 1936 production
Courtesy: Douglas Lanier

119: **idolatry:** excessive veneration

My true love's passion; therefore, pardon me,
And not impute this yielding to light love,
' Which the dark night hath so discoverèd.   110

ROMEO
Lady, by yonder blessed moon I swear
That tips with silver all these fruit-tree tops —

JULIET
O, swear not by the moon, th' inconstant moon,
That monthly changes in her circled orb,
Lest that thy love prove likewise variable.   115

ROMEO
What shall I swear by?

JULIET
                        Do not swear at all.
Or, if thou wilt, swear by thy gracious self,
Which is the god of my idolatry,
And I'll believe thee.   120

ROMEO
If my heart's dear love —

JULIET
Well, do not swear. Although I joy in thee,
I have no joy of this contract tonight.
It is too rash, too unadvised, too sudden,
Too like the lightning, which doth cease to be   125
Ere one can say, "It lightens." Sweet, good night.
This bud of love, by summer's ripening breath,
May prove a beauteous flower when next we meet.
Good night, good night. As sweet repose and rest
Come to thy heart as that within my breast.   130

ROMEO
O, wilt thou leave me so unsatisfied?

137: **frank:** liberal, bountiful

138: **but:** only

149: **bent:** leaning or bias of the mind

JULIET
What satisfaction canst thou have tonight?

ROMEO
Th' exchange of thy love's faithful vow for mine.

JULIET
I gave thee mine before thou didst request it,
And yet I would it were to give again. 135

ROMEO
Wouldst thou withdraw it? For what purpose, love?

JULIET
But to be frank, and give it thee again.
And yet I wish but for the thing I have.
My bounty is as boundless as the sea;
My love as deep. The more I give to thee, 140
The more I have, for both are infinite.

[*NURSE calls within*]

I hear some noise within. Dear love, adieu. —
Anon, good nurse! — Sweet Montague, be true.
Stay but a little, I will come again.

[*Exit, above*]

ROMEO
O blessèd, blessèd night. I am afeard, 145
Being in night, all this is but a dream,
Too flattering sweet to be substantial.

[*Re-enter JULIET, above*]

JULIET
Three words, dear Romeo, and good night indeed.
If that thy bent of love be honourable,
Thy purpose marriage, send me word tomorrow, 150
By one that I'll procure to come to thee,
Where and what time thou wilt perform the rite,
And all my fortunes at thy foot I'll lay
And follow thee my lord throughout the world.

162: **So thrive my soul:** a form of solemn assurance

167: **falconer's voice:** "The good falconer's voice," according to eminent Victorian explorer Sir Richard Francis Burton, "must be sweet and clear as a bell, for falcons fear and hate a shrill, harsh, or loud sound."

168: **tassel-gentle:** tiercel-gentle, a male falcon

170: **Echo:** from mythology, a nymph who pines away for Narcissus till only her voice remains, doomed to repeat what others say

NURSE

[*Within*]

   Madam! 155

JULIET
   I come, anon. — But if thou mean'st not well,
   I do beseech thee —

NURSE

[*Within*]

   Madam!

JULIET
          By and by, I come. —
   To cease thy suit, and leave me to my grief. 160
   Tomorrow will I send.

ROMEO
          So thrive my soul —

JULIET
   A thousand times good night.

[*Exit, above*]

ROMEO
   A thousand times the worse, to want thy light.
   Love goes toward love, as schoolboys from their books, 165
   But love from love, toward school with heavy looks.

[*Retiring*]
[*Enter JULIET again*]

JULIET
   Hist, Romeo, hist! O, for a falconer's voice
   To lure this tassel-gentle back again.
   Bondage is hoarse and may not speak aloud;
   Else would I tear the cave where Echo lies,
   And make her airy tongue more hoarse than mine, 170
   With repetition of my Romeo's name.

Line 182: "I have forgot why I did call thee back": Olivia Hussey as Juliet and
Leonard Whiting as Romeo in Franco Zeffirelli's 1968 movie production
Courtesy: Douglas Lanier

189: **wanton:** one apt to play and dally

191: **gyves:** chains, fetters

ROMEO
  It is my soul that calls upon my name.
  How silver-sweet sound lovers' tongues by night,
  Like softest music to attending ears.   175

JULIET
  Romeo!

ROMEO
  My dear?

JULIET
  What o'clock tomorrow
  Shall I send to thee?

ROMEO
  By the hour of nine.   180

JULIET
  I will not fail. 'Tis twenty years till then.
  I have forgot why I did call thee back.

ROMEO
  Let me stand here till thou remember it.

JULIET
  I shall forget, to have thee still stand there,
  Rememb'ring how I love thy company.   185

ROMEO
  And I'll still stay, to have thee still forget,
  Forgetting any other home but this.

JULIET
  'Tis almost morning. I would have thee gone,
  And yet no further than a wanton's bird,
  That lets it hop a little from his hand,   190
  Like a poor prisoner in his twisted gyves,
  And with a silken thread plucks it back again,
  So loving-jealous of his liberty.

201: **ghostly:** spiritual

201: **close:** confined; free from observation

202: **crave:** beg

202: **dear hap:** good fortune

ROMEO
I would I were thy bird.

JULIET
              Sweet, so would I.   195
Yet I should kill thee with much cherishing.
Good night, good night. Parting is such sweet sorrow,
That I shall say good night till it be morrow.

                                  [Exit above]

ROMEO
Sleep dwell upon thine eyes, peace in thy breast.
Would I were sleep and peace, so sweet to rest   200
Hence will I to my ghostly friar's close cell,
His help to crave, and my dear hap to tell.

                                          [Exit]

4: **Titan:** god of the sun

4: **fiery wheels:** i.e., the sun (In Greek and Roman mythology, the sun god drives his fiery chariot across the sky to represent the sun.)

7: **osier cage:** willow basket

11: **divers kind:** different kinds

15: **mickle:** great, powerful

30: **canker:** maggot, worm

Act 2: Scene 3]

[*Enter FRIAR LAURENCE, with a basket*]

FRIAR LAURENCE
  The grey-eyed morn smiles on the frowning night,
  Check'ring the eastern clouds with streaks of light,
  And flecked darkness like a drunkard reels
  From forth day's path and Titan's fiery wheels.
  Now, ere the sun advance his burning eye,   5
  The day to cheer and night's dank dew to dry,
  I must upfill this osier cage of ours
  With baleful weeds and precious-juiced flowers.
  The earth that's nature's mother is her tomb;
  What is her burying grave, that is her womb;   10
  And from her womb, children of divers kind
  We sucking on her natural bosom find,
  Many for many, virtues excellent,
  None but for some, and yet all different.
  O, mickle is the powerful grace that lies   15
  In plants, herbs, stones, and their true qualities:
  For nought so vile that on the earth doth live,
  But to the earth some special good doth give,
  Nor aught so good but strained from that fair use,
  Revolts from true birth, stumbling on abuse.   20
  Virtue itself turns vice, being misapplied,
  And vice sometimes by action dignified.
  Within the infant rind of this weak flower
  Poison hath residence and medicine power.
  For this, being smelt, with that part cheers each part;   25
  Being tasted, slays all senses with the heart.
  Two such opposèd kings encamp them still,
  In man as well as herbs, grace and rude will;
  And where the worser is predominant,
  Full soon the canker death eats up that plant.   30

[*Enter ROMEO*]

32: **Benedicite:** salutation used by friars

34: **distempered:** distracted, disturbed

41: **distemp'rature:** (distemperature) disorder of the mind

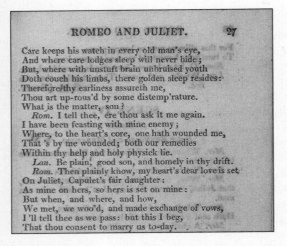

ROMEO AND JULIET.   27

Care keeps his watch in every old man's eye,
And where care lodges sleep will never bide;
But, where with unstuft brain unbruised youth
Doth couch his limbs, there golden sleep resides:
Therefore thy earliness assureth me,
Thou art up-rous'd by some distemp'rature.
What is the matter, son?
    Rom. I tell thee, ere thou ask it me again.
I have been feasting with mine enemy;
Where, to the heart's core, one hath wounded me,
That's by me wounded; both our remedies
Within thy help and holy physick lie.
    Lau. Be plain, good son, and homely in thy drift.
    Rom. Then plainly know, my heart's dear love is set
On Juliet, Capulet's fair daughter:
As mine on hers, so hers is set on mine:
But when, and where, and how,
We met, we woo'd, and made exchange of vows,
I'll tell thee as we pass: but this I beg,
That thou consent to marry us to-day.

Since Rosaline is not in J. P. Kemble's production, lines 42–48, the exchange
between the Friar and Romeo, have been been replaced with the single line,
"What is the matter, son?"

53: **physic:** the art of healing diseases

55: **steads:** helps, assists

ROMEO
    Good morrow, father.

FRIAR LAURENCE
                    Benedicite.
    What early tongue so sweet saluteth me?
    Young son, it argues a distempered head
    So soon to bid good morrow to thy bed.   35
    Care keeps his watch in every old man's eye,
    And where care lodges, sleep will never lie;
    But where unbruisèd youth with unstuffed brain
    Doth couch his limbs, there golden sleep doth reign.
    Therefore thy earliness doth me assure   40
    Thou art uproused by some distemp'rature;
    Or if not so, then here I hit it right,
    Our Romeo hath not been in bed tonight.

ROMEO
    That last is true; the sweeter rest was mine.

FRIAR LAURENCE
    God pardon sin! Wast thou with Rosaline?   45

ROMEO
    With Rosaline, my ghostly father? No.
    I have forgot that name, and that name's woe.

FRIAR LAURENCE
    That's my good son, but where hast thou been then?

ROMEO
    I'll tell thee, ere thou ask it me again.
    I have been feasting with mine enemy,   50
    Where on a sudden one hath wounded me
    That's by me wounded. Both our remedies
    Within thy help and holy physic lies.
    I bear no hatred, blessèd man, for, lo,
    My intercession likewise steads my foe.   55

56: **homely in thy drift:** plainspoken

57: **shrift:** absolution

70: **brine:** tears

81: **may fall:** may sin

82: **chid'st me oft:** scolded me often

Line 83: "For doting, not for loving, pupil mine": Leonard Whiting as Romeo and Milo O'Shea as Friar Laurence in Franco Zeffirelli's 1968 movie production
Courtesy: Douglas Lanier

FRIAR LAURENCE
    Be plain, good son, and homely in thy drift;
    Riddling confession finds but riddling shrift.

ROMEO
    Then plainly know my heart's dear love is set
    On the fair daughter of rich Capulet.
    As mine on hers, so hers is set on mine,   60
    And all combined, save what thou must combine
    By holy marriage. When and where and how
    We met, we wooed, and made exchange of vow,
    I'll tell thee as we pass, but this I pray,
    That thou consent to marry us today.   65

FRIAR LAURENCE
    Holy Saint Francis, what a change is here!
    Is Rosaline, whom thou didst love so dear
    So soon forsaken? Young men's love then lies
    Not truly in their hearts, but in their eyes.
    Jesu Maria, what a deal of brine   70
    Hath washed thy sallow cheeks for Rosaline!
    How much salt water thrown away in waste,
    To season love, that of it doth not taste.
    The sun not yet thy sighs from heaven clears,
    Thy old groans ring yet in my ancient ears.   75
    Lo, here upon thy cheek the stain doth sit
    Of an old tear that is not washed off yet.
    If e'er thou wast thyself and these woes thine,
    Thou and these woes were all for Rosaline.
    And art thou changed? Pronounce this sentence then: 80
    "Women may fall, when there's no strength in men."

ROMEO
    Thou chid'st me oft for loving Rosaline.

FRIAR LAURENCE
    For doting, not for loving, pupil mine.

84: **bad'st me:** told me to

91: **Thy love…not spell:** you do not really understand love and are only repeating what you have heard

ROMEO
    And bad'st me bury love.

FRIAR LAURENCE
                    Not in a grave,   85
    To lay one in, another out to have.

ROMEO
    I pray thee, chide me not. Her I love now
    Doth grace for grace and love for love allow.
    The other did not so.

FRIAR LAURENCE
                    O, she knew well   90
    Thy love did read by rote and could not spell.
    But come, young waverer, come, go with me.
    In one respect I'll thy assistant be,
    For this alliance may so happy prove
    To turn your households' rancour to pure love.   95

ROMEO
    O, let us hence. I stand on sudden haste.

FRIAR LAURENCE
    Wisely and slow; they stumble that run fast.

                                        [*Exeunt*]

14: **pin:** center of a target

14: **cleft:** cut in two

14: **blind bow-boy:** i.e., Cupid

14: **butt-shaft:** a kind of arrow used for archery practice

Act 2: Scene 4]

[*Enter BENVOLIO and MERCUTIO*]

MERCUTIO
Where the devil should this Romeo be?
Came he not home tonight?

BENVOLIO
Not to his father's; I spoke with his man.

MERCUTIO
Why, that same pale hard-hearted wench, that Rosaline,
Torments him so that he will sure run mad.   5

BENVOLIO
Tybalt, the kinsman to old Capulet,
Hath sent a letter to his father's house.

MERCUTIO
A challenge, on my life.

BENVOLIO
Romeo will answer it.

MERCUTIO
Any man that can write may answer a letter.   10

BENVOLIO
Nay, he will answer the letter's master how he dares, being dared.

MERCUTIO
Alas poor Romeo! He is already dead, stabbed with a white
wench's black eye, run through the ear with a love song, the very
pin of his heart cleft with the blind bow-boy's butt-shaft. And is
he a man to encounter Tybalt?   15

17: **prince of cats:** Tybalt was the name of the cat in *The History of Reynard the Fox*

18: **compliments:** formal civility or courtesy

18: **prick-song:** harmony that is written down or pricked down as opposed to plain-song, sung extemporaneously

19: **minim:** a very short moment (referring to *minum*, the shortest note in music)

21: **first house:** best, noblest family

The following four terms are from duelling, fashionable in that time:

21–22: **first and second cause:** (according to the dueling code) causes obliging one to make a challenge and seek satisfaction

22: **passado:** a forward thrust, accompanied by a pass

22: **punto reverso:** a reverse thrust made from the left side with the hand in supination (knuckles down, palm inward)

22: **hai:** (Italian *hai,* meaning "you have it") an exclamation made when a thrust or hit is received by the antagonist

24: **antic:** odd

28: **perdona-mi's:** (Italian *perdona mi*, meaning "pardon me") overly polite people

28: **stand:** insist

28: **form:** established practice

29: **bones:** pun on French *bon,* meaning "good"

31: **Without his roe:** (1) Without the first syllable of his name ("roe" = "Ro"), we are left with "meo," which sounds like a lover's sigh (2) sexual connation: sexually spent (Mercutio then picks up "roe" – fish eggs – to joke about fish, extending the sexual pun.)

32: **numbers:** verses, i.e., Romeo is patterning his behavior after love poems

32: **Petrarch:** famous 14th century Italian poet

33: **Laura:** the object of Petrarch's love sonnets

34: **Dido:** Dido, Queen of Carthage, had an ill-fated love affair with Aeneas, Prince of Troy

34: **dowdy:** loose woman

34: **Cleopatra:** Queen of Egypt, has an ill-fated love affair with Antony that ends with their deaths

34: **Helen:** Helen of Troy, whose remarkable beauty precipitated the Trojan war

35: **Hero:** beloved of Leander, tragic lovers of Greek mythology

35: **hilding:** a degenerate wretch

35: **Thisbe:** beloved of Pyramus, tragic lovers of Greek mythology

37: **french slop:** large, loose trousers

37: **gave us the counterfeit:** gave us the slip

BENVOLIO
Why, what is Tybalt?

MERCUTIO
More than prince of cats. O, he's the courageous captain of
compliments. He fights as you sing prick-song, keeps time,
distance, and proportion. He rests his minim rests, one, two, and
the third in your bosom; the very butcher of a silk button, a duelist,   20
a duelist, a gentleman of the very first house of the first and second
cause. Ah, the immortal passado! The punto reverso! The hai!

BENVOLIO
The what?

MERCUTIO
The pox of such antic, lisping, affecting fantasies; these new tuners of
accent! "By Jesu, a very good blade! a very tall man! A very good   25
whore!" Why, is not this a lamentable thing, grandsire, that we should
be thus afflicted with these strange flies, these fashion-mongers, these
perdona-mi's, who stand so much on the new form that they cannot
sit at ease on the old bench? O, their bones, their bones!

                                                    [*Enter ROMEO*]

BENVOLIO
Here comes Romeo, here comes Romeo.   30

MERCUTIO
Without his roe, like a dried herring. O flesh, flesh, how art thou
fishified? Now is he for the numbers that Petrarch flowed in:
Laura to his lady was a kitchen-wench (marry, she had a better
love to berhyme her) Dido a dowdy; Cleopatra a gypsy; Helen and
Hero hildings and harlots; Thisbe a grey eye or so, but not to the   35
purpose. Signior Romeo, bonjour! There's a French salutation to
your French slop. You gave us the counterfeit fairly last night.

ROMEO
Good morrow to you both. What counterfeit did I give you?

MERCUTIO
The slip, sir, the slip; can you not conceive?

43: **bow in the hams:** a deep, bent-legged bow (hams = hamstrings)

Lines 42–43: "Such a case as yours / constrains a man to bow in the hams":
Courtney B. Vance as Mercutio and Peter MacNicol as Romeo in the Public Theater's
1987–88 production directed by Les Waters
Photo: George E. Joseph

47: **pink of courtesy:** paragon (pink) of good manners with a pun on curtsey

50: **pump:** shoe

50: **well flowered:** ornamented with flowers

53: **solely singular:** both unique and solitary

54: **single-soled:** silly, contemptible

54: **singleness:** silliness

ROMEO
    Pardon, good Mercutio, my business was great, and in   40
    such a case as mine, a man may strain courtesy.

MERCUTIO
    That's as much as to say, such a case as yours
    constrains a man to bow in the hams.

ROMEO
    Meaning, to curtsy.

MERCUTIO
    Thou hast most kindly hit it.   45

ROMEO
    A most courteous exposition.

MERCUTIO
    Nay, I am the very pink of courtesy.

ROMEO
    Pink for flower.

MERCUTIO
    Right.

ROMEO
    Why, then is my pump well flowered.   50

MERCUTIO
    Sure wit, follow me this jest now till thou hast worn out thy pump, that
    when the single sole of it is worn, the jest may remain after the wearing
    solely singular.

ROMEO
    O single-soled jest, solely singular for the singleness.

MERCUTIO
    Come between us, good Benvolio; my wits faints.   55

56: **switch and spurs:** Romeo spurs Mercutio on in their battle of wits

56: **cry a match:** declare victory

57: **wild goose chase:** race between two horses, with the leader choosing the course

59: **five:** wits

59: **Was I...the goose?:** i.e., did I outwit you?

61, 63: **goose:** prostitute or silly person (Romeo implies both)

64: **bitter sweeting:** kind of sweet apple

66: **cheveril:** roebuck-leather; symbol of flexibility

66–67: **ell broad:** forty-five inches long

69: **broad goose:** (broad = plain, evident) i.e., foolish

72: **driveling:** doting, foolish

73: **lolling:** with the tongue sticking out

73: **bauble in a hole:** bauble = useless plaything (with sexual innuendo)

ROMEO
Switch and spurs, switch and spurs, or I'll cry a match.

MERCUTIO
Nay, if thy wits run the wild goose chase, I am done, for thou hast more
of the wild goose in one of thy wits than, I am sure, I have in my whole
five. Was I with you there for the goose?

ROMEO
Thou wast never with me for anything when thou wast not there   60
for the goose.

MERCUTIO
I will bite thee by the ear for that jest.

ROMEO
Nay, good goose, bite not.

MERCUTIO
Thy wit is a very bitter sweeting; it is a most sharp sauce.

ROMEO
And is it not then well served into a sweet goose?   65

MERCUTIO
O here's a wit of cheveril that stretches from an inch narrow to an ell
broad.

ROMEO
I stretch it out for that word "broad," which, added to the goose, proves
thee far and wide a broad goose.

MERCUTIO
Why, is not this better now than groaning for love? Now art thou   70
sociable, now art thou Romeo, now art thou what thou art, by art
as well as by nature. For this driveling love is like a great natural
that runs lolling up and down to hide his bauble in a hole.

BENVOLIO
Stop there, stop there.

75: **against the hair:** against my inclination (with sexual innuendo)

76: **thy tale:** your story (also a pun on "your tail," the male sex organ. Mercutio picks up this pun in his next lines.)

78: **occupy:** interact with but also: fornicate

80: **goodly gear:** fine items

82: **a shirt and a smock:** a man and a woman (shirt = man's undergarment; smock = woman's undergarment)

MERCUTIO
Thou desirest me to stop in my tale against the hair.   75

BENVOLIO
Thou wouldst else have made thy tale large.

MERCUTIO
O, thou art deceived. I would have made it short, for I was come to the whole depth of my tale and meant, indeed, to occupy the argument no longer.

ROMEO
Here's goodly gear.   80
[Enter NURSE and her man, PETER]

A sail, a sail!

MERCUTIO
Two, two. A shirt and a smock.

NURSE
Peter!

PETER
Anon!

NURSE
My fan, Peter.   85

MERCUTIO
Good Peter, to hide her face, for her fan's the fairer face.

NURSE
God ye good morrow, gentlemen.

MERCUTIO
God ye good den, fair gentlewoman.

NURSE
Is it good den?

90: **dial:** clock (with a bawdy inference because the hand points straight up)

91: **prick:** mark on a clock (with sexual pun)

94: **quoth he:** says he

98: **for fault:** for want

98: **worse:** i.e., a worse name

102: **indite:** invite

103: **bawd:** procurer or procuress (also a north midland word for *hare*)

Line 103: "A bawd, a bawd, a bawd! So ho!": John Barrymore as Mercutio, Edna May Oliver as Nurse, and Leslie Howard as Romeo in George Cukor's 1936 movie production
Courtesy: Douglas Lanier

105: **hare:** slang for prostitute

106: **hoar:** moldy; pun on *whore*

MERCUTIO
'Tis no less, I tell you, for the bawdy hand of the dial is now upon   90
the prick of noon.

NURSE
Out upon you! What a man are you!

ROMEO
One, gentlewoman, that God hath made for himself to mar.

NURSE
By my troth, it is well said, "for himself to mar," quoth he? Gentlemen,
can any of you tell me where I may find the young Romeo?   95

ROMEO
I can tell you, but young Romeo will be older when you have
found him than he was when you sought him. I am the youngest
of that name, for fault of a worse.

NURSE
You say well.

MERCUTIO
Yea, is the worst well? Very well took, i' faith, wisely, wisely.   100

NURSE
If you be he, sir, I desire some confidence with you.

BENVOLIO
She will indite him to some supper.

MERCUTIO
A bawd, a bawd, a bawd! So ho!

ROMEO
What hast thou found?

MERCUTIO
No hare, sir, unless a hare, sir, in a lenten pie, that is something   105
stale and hoar ere it be spent.

117: **ropery:** roguish mischief

119: **stand to:** put up with

120: **an a':** if he

122: **scurvy knave:** vile scoundrel

122: **flirt-gills:** women of loose behavior

123: **skains-mates:** editors are unsure of the meaning; suggestions include *cut-throats* (Applause Acting Edition) and *daggermates, outlaws,* or *gangster molls* (Bevington in The Complete Works of Shakespeare, Fifth Edition)

[*Sings*]

> *An old hare hoar,*
> *And an old hare hoar,*
> *Is very good meat in lent*
> *But a hare that is hoar*   110
> *Is too much for a score,*
> *When it hoars ere it be spent.*

Romeo, will you come to your father's? We'll to dinner, thither.

ROMEO
   I will follow you.

MERCUTIO
   Farewell, ancient lady. Farewell, lady, lady, lady.   115
   [*Exeunt MERCUTIO and BENVOLIO*]

NURSE
   I pray you, sir, what saucy merchant was this that was so full of
   his ropery?

ROMEO
   A gentleman, nurse, that loves to hear himself talk and will speak
   more in a minute than he will stand to in a month.

NURSE
   An a' speak anything against me, I'll take him down, an a' were   120
   lustier than he is and twenty such Jacks, and if I cannot, I'll find
   those that shall. Scurvy knave, I am none of his flirt-gills, I am
   none of his skains-mates. And thou must stand by too and suffer
   every knave to use me at his pleasure.

PETER
   I saw no man use you at his pleasure. If I had, my weapon should   125
   quickly have been out, I warrant you. I dare draw as soon as another
   man, if I see occasion in a good quarrel and the law on my side.

NURSE
   Now, afore God, I am so vexed that every part about me quivers,
   scurvy knave. — Pray you, sir, a word. And as I told you, my

135: weak: contemptible

143: shrift: confession

145: be shrived: have confessed and been absolved

Line 149: "And stay, good nurse, behind the abbey wall": Peter MacNicol as Romeo and Anne Meara as the Nurse in the Public Theater's 1988 production directed by Les Waters

Photo: George E. Joseph

young lady bid me inquire you out. What she bid me say, I will   130
keep to myself. But first let me tell ye, if ye should lead her into a
fool's paradise, as they say, it were a very gross kind of behavior,
as they say. For the gentlewoman is young, and therefore, if you
should deal double with her, truly it were an ill thing to be offered
to any gentlewoman, and very weak dealing.   135

ROMEO
Nurse, commend me to thy lady and mistress. I protest unto thee.

NURSE
Good heart, and, i' faith, I will tell her as much. — Lord, Lord,
she will be a joyful woman.

ROMEO
What wilt thou tell her, nurse? Thou dost not mark me.

NURSE
I will tell her, sir, that you do protest, which, as I take it, is a   140
gentlemanlike offer.

ROMEO
Bid her devise
Some means to come to shrift this afternoon,
And there she shall at Friar Laurence' cell
Be shrived and married. Here is for thy pains.   145

NURSE
No, truly sir, not a penny.

ROMEO
Go to; I say you shall.

NURSE
This afternoon, sir? Well, she shall be there.

ROMEO
And stay, good nurse, behind the abbey wall.
Within this hour my man shall be with thee   150

151: **cords:** ropes

151: **tackled stair:** rope-ladder

152: **top-gallant:** summit, pinnacle

153: **convoy:** conveyance

154: **quit:** reward

159: **Two may...one away:** a proverb (a Benjamin Franklin paraphrase is, "Three may keep a secret if two of them are dead.")

162: **prating:** chattering

163: **fain:** gladly, willingly

163: **lay knife aboard:** lay claim to her

164: **lief:** should like as much to

166: **clout:** cloth, linen

166: **versal world:** universe

167: **with a letter:** i.e., with the same letter

169: **the dog's name:** R approximates the sound of a growling dog.

170: **sententious:** modern editors agree that the nurse meant to say *sentences*, meaning maxims, or pithy sayings

And bring thee cords made like a tackled stair,
Which to the high top-gallant of my joy
Must be my convoy in the secret night.
Farewell. Be trusty, and I'll quit thy pains.
Farewell. Commend me to thy mistress.   155

NURSE
Now God in heaven bless thee! Hark you, sir.

ROMEO
What say'st thou, my dear nurse?

NURSE
Is your man secret? Did you ne'er hear say,
Two may keep counsel, putting one away?

ROMEO
I warrant thee, my man's as true as steel.   160

NURSE
Well, sir, my mistress is the sweetest lady — Lord, Lord, when
'twas a little prating thing — O, there is a nobleman in town, one
Paris, that would fain lay knife aboard, but she, good soul, had as
lief see a toad, a very toad, as see him. I anger her sometimes and
tell her that Paris is the properer man, but, I'll warrant you, when   165
I say so, she looks as pale as any clout in the versal world. Doth
not rosemary and Romeo begin both with a letter?

ROMEO
Ay, nurse, what of that? Both with an R.

NURSE
A mocker, that's the dog's name. R is for the — No, I know it begins
with some other letter. — And she hath the prettiest sententious of   170
it, of you and rosemary, that it would do you good to hear it.

ROMEO
Commend me to thy lady.

176: **apace:** at a quick pace

ROMEO AND JULIET.   31

Nurse. Good heart! and, i' faith, I will tell her as
much :—Lord, lord! she will be a joyful woman.
Rom. What wilt thou tell her, nurse? Thou dost
not mark me.
Nurse. I will tell her, sir,—that you do protest;
which, as I take it, is a very gentleman-like offer.
Rom. Bid her devise some means to come to shrift
This afternoon;
And there she shall, at friar Laurence' cell,
Be shriv'd, and married.—Here is for thy pains.
Nurse. No truly, sir; not a penny.
Rom. Go to; I say, you shall.
Nurse. This afternoon, sir? Well, she shall be there.
Rom. And stay, good nurse, behind the abbey wall:
Within this hour my man shall be with thee,
And bring thee cords made like a tackled stair;
Which to the high top-gallant of my joy
Must be my convoy in the secret night.
Farewell! Be trusty, and I 'll quit thy pains.
Nurse. Well, sir, my mistress is the sweetest lady,
—Lord, lord! when 'twas a little prating thing,
O,—there 's a nobleman in town, one Paris, that would
fain lay knife aboard: but she, good soul, had as lieve
see a toad, a very toad, as see him.—I anger her some-
times, and tell her that Paris is the properer man:
but, I 'll warrant you, when I say so, she looks as pale
as any clout in the versal world.
Rom. Commend me to thy lady.   [*Exit* ROMEO. R M
Nurse. Ay,—a thousand times.—Peter!
Pet. Anon?
Nurse. Peter, take my fan, and go before.
                                   [*Exeunt.* S M

D 2

J. P. Kemble cuts the Nurse's lnes about Paris being Juliet's suitor.
He also alters Paris's lines when Paris and Romeo meet at the Capulet monument,
removing references to Juliet and Paris's love.

NURSE
  Ay, a thousand times.

                                              [*Exit Romeo*]

  Peter!

PETER
  Anon!   175

NURSE
  Before and apace.

                                              [*Exeunt*]

7: **nimble-pinioned:** swift-winged

14: **bandy her:** move her to and fro, as a ball

Act 2: Scene 5]

[*Enter JULIET*]

JULIET
  The clock struck nine when I did send the nurse.
  In half an hour she promised to return.
  Perchance she cannot meet him. That's not so.
  O, she is lame! Love's heralds should be thoughts,
  Which ten times faster glide than the sun's beams,   5
  Driving back shadows over louring hills.
  Therefore do nimble-pinioned doves draw love,
  And therefore hath the wind-swift Cupid wings.
  Now is the sun upon the highmost hill
  Of this day's journey, and from nine till twelve   10
  Is three long hours, yet she is not come.
  Had she affections and warm youthful blood,
  She would be as swift in motion as a ball.
  My words would bandy her to my sweet love,
  And his to me.   15
  But old folks, many feign as they were dead,
  Unwieldy, slow, heavy and pale as lead.

[*Enter NURSE and PETER*]

  O God, she comes!   O honey nurse, what news?
  Hast thou met with him? Send thy man away.

NURSE
  Peter, stay at the gate.   20

[*Exit PETER*]

JULIET
  Now, good sweet Nurse, — O Lord, why look'st thou sad?
  Though news be sad, yet tell them merrily.
  If good, thou shamest the music of sweet news
  By playing it to me with so sour a face.
NURSE

26: **jaunt:** tiring journey

29: **stay:** wait

36: **stay the circumstance:** wait for the details

48: **o' t' other:** contraction for "on the other"

49: **beshrew:** woe to

I am a-weary, give me leave awhile.   25
Fie, how my bones ache! What a jaunt have I!

NURSE

I would thou hadst my bones, and I thy news.
Nay, come, I pray thee, speak. Good, good nurse, speak.

NURSE

Jesu, what haste? Can you not stay awhile?
Do you not see that I am out of breath?   30

JULIET

How art thou out of breath, when thou hast breath
To say to me that thou art out of breath?
The excuse that thou dost make in this delay
Is longer than the tale thou dost excuse.
Is thy news good or bad? Answer to that.   35
Say either, and I'll stay the circumstance.
Let me be satisfied; is't good or bad?

NURSE

Well, you have made a simple choice; you know not how to choose
a man. Romeo, no, not he though his face be better than any man's,
yet his leg excels all men's, and for a hand and a foot and a body,
though they be not to be talked on, yet they are past compare. He is   40
not the flower of courtesy, but, I'll warrant him, as gentle as a lamb.
Go thy ways, wench; serve God. What, have you dined at home?

JULIET

No, no, but all this did I know before.
What says he of our marriage? What of that?   45

NURSE

Lord, how my head aches! What a head have I!
It beats as it would fall in twenty pieces.
My back, o' t' other side. — Ah, my back, my back!
Beshrew your heart for sending me about
To catch my death with jaunting up and down!   50
JULIET

61: **hot:** excited, excitable

61: **I trow:** I dare say

62: **poultice:** salve

64: **coil:** fuss

67: **hie:** hurry

74: **drudge:** servant

I' faith, I am sorry that thou art not well.
Sweet, sweet, sweet nurse, tell me, what says my love?

NURSE
Your love says, like an honest gentleman, and a
courteous, and a kind, and a handsome, and, I
warrant, a virtuous, — Where is your mother?   55

JULIET
Where is my mother! Why, she is within;
Where should she be? How oddly thou repliest!
"Your love says, like an honest gentleman,
Where is your mother?"

NURSE
               O God's lady dear!   60
Are you so hot? Marry, come up, I trow,
Is this the poultice for my aching bones?
Henceforward do your messages yourself.

JULIET
Here's such a coil. Come, what says Romeo?

NURSE
Have you got leave to go to shrift today?   65

JULIET
I have.

NURSE
Then hie you hence to Friar Laurence' cell.
There stays a husband to make you a wife.
Now comes the wanton blood up in your cheeks;
They'll be in scarlet straight at any news.   70
Hie you to church; I must another way
To fetch a ladder, by the which your love
Must climb a bird's nest soon when it is dark.
I am the drudge and toil in your delight,
But you shall bear the burden soon at night.   75

77: **hie:** make haste

Line 77: "Hie to high fortune. Honest Nurse, farewell": Edna May Oliver as the
Nurse and Norma Shearer as Juliet in George Cukor's 1936 production
Courtesy: Douglas Lanier

Go. I'll to dinner; hie you to the cell.

JULIET
Hie to high fortune. Honest Nurse, farewell.

[Exeunt]

4: **countervail:** balance

13: **confounds:** ruins

17: **everlasting flint:** cobblestones

18: **gossamer:** white filaments, like cobwebs

Act 2: Scene 6]

[Enter FRIAR LAURENCE and ROMEO]

FRIAR LAURENCE
So smile the heavens upon this holy act,
That after hours, with sorrow chide us not!

ROMEO
Amen, amen, but come what sorrow can,
It cannot countervail the exchange of joy
That one short minute gives me in her sight.   5
Do thou but close our hands with holy words,
Then love-devouring death do what he dare.
It is enough I may but call her mine.

FRIAR LAURENCE
These violent delights have violent ends,
And in their triumph die, like fire and powder,   10
Which, as they kiss, consume. The sweetest honey
Is loathsome in his own deliciousness
And in the taste confounds the appetite.
Therefore, love moderately. Long love doth so.
Too swift arrives as tardy as too slow.   15
[Enter JULIET]

Here comes the lady. O, so light a foot
Will ne'er wear out the everlasting flint.
A lover may bestride the gossamers
That idles in the wanton summer air
And yet not fall, so light is vanity.   20

JULIET
Good even to my ghostly confessor.

FRIAR LAURENCE
Romeo shall thank thee, daughter, for us both.

Lines 24–25: "Ah, Juliet, if the measure of thy joy / Be heaped like mine": Susan McArthur as Juliet and Martin Sheen as Romeo in the Public Theater's 1967–68 production directed by Joseph Papp and Edward Cornell
Photo: George E. Joseph

26: **blazon:** trumpet, praise

27: **neighbour air:** air around us

30: **conceit:** understanding

37: **incorporate two in one:** join in marriage

JULIET
  As much to him, else is his thanks too much.

ROMEO
  Ah, Juliet, if the measure of thy joy
  Be heaped like mine and that thy skill be more   25
  To blazon it, then sweeten with thy breath
  This neighbour air, and let rich music's tongue
  Unfold the imagined happiness that both
  Receive in either by this dear encounter.

JULIET
  Conceit, more rich in matter than in words,   30
  Brags of his substance, not of ornament.
  They are but beggars that can count their worth,
  But my true love is grown to such excess
  I cannot sum up sum of half my wealth.

FRIAR LAURENCE
  Come, come with me, and we will make short work.   35
  For, by your leaves, you shall not stay alone
  Till holy church incorporate two in one.

                                                      [*Exeunt*]

[Romeo and Juliet

Act 3

Stage direction: **Enter MERCUTIO, BENVOLIO, and men:** Kyle Kenzler (Mercutio), Will Sturdivant (Abram), Nathan Christopher (Page to Mercutio), and Michael Chernus (Benvolio) in the Guthrie Theater's 2004 production directed by Ethan McSweeny

Photo: Michal Daniel

3: **scape:** escape

6: **claps me his sword:** strikes a surface with his sword (an aggressive gesture)

8: **drawer:** waiter

11: **moody:** peevish, angry

19: **addle:** rotten

Act 3: Scene 1]

[*Enter MERCUTIO, BENVOLIO, and men*]

BENVOLIO
I pray thee, good Mercutio, let's retire.
The day is hot, the Capulets abroad,
And, if we meet, we shall not scape a brawl,
For now, these hot days, is the mad blood stirring.

MERCUTIO
Thou art like one of those fellows that when he enters the confines   5
of a tavern claps me his sword upon the table and says, "God send
me no need of thee!" and by the operation of the second cup,
draws it on the drawer, when indeed there is no need.

BENVOLIO
Am I like such a fellow?

MERCUTIO
Come, come, thou art as hot a Jack in thy mood as any in Italy,   10
and as soon moved to be moody, and as soon moody to be moved.

BENVOLIO
And what to?

MERCUTIO
Nay, an there were two such, we should have none shortly, for one
would kill the other. Thou! Why, thou wilt quarrel with a man that
hath a hair more, or a hair less, in his beard than thou hast. Thou   15
wilt quarrel with a man for cracking nuts, having no other reason
but because thou hast hazel eyes. What eye but such an eye would
spy out such a quarrel? Thy head is as full of quarrels as an egg is
full of meat, and yet thy head hath been beaten as addle as an egg
for quarreling. Thou hast quarreled with a man for coughing in   20
the street, because he hath wakened thy dog that hath lain asleep

23: **doublet:** close-fitting body-garment worn by men from the 14th to the 18th century

24: **riband:** ribbon

26: **fee-simple:** hereditary and unconditional property (implying something of value)

27: **simple:** stupid, ridiculous

34: **an:** if

36: **thou consortest:** you consort, meaning pass the time or keep company with (archaic verb form)

37: **minstrel:** one who sings and makes music for money

38: **discords:** bad notes (pun on arguments)

38: **fiddlestick:** i.e., his sword (and probably also a rude sexual suggestion)

39: **Zounds:** an oath contracted from God's wounds (Swounds)

39: **consort:** keep company or maintain a fellowship, as in a band of lower class musicians (Mercutio has deliberately taken this as an insult)

in the sun. Didst thou not fall out with a tailor for wearing his new doublet before Easter? With another, for tying his new shoes with old riband? And yet thou wilt tutor me from quarrelling?

BENVOLIO
An I were so apt to quarrel as thou art, any man should buy the   25
fee-simple of my life for an hour and a quarter.

MERCUTIO
The fee-simple. O simple.

[Enter TYBALT and others]

BENVOLIO
By my head, here come the Capulets.

MERCUTIO
By my heel, I care not.

TYBALT
Follow me close, for I will speak to them. —   30
Gentlemen, good den. A word with one of you.

MERCUTIO
And but one word with one of us? Couple it with something; make it a word and a blow.

TYBALT
You shall find me apt enough to that, sir, an you will give me occasion.

MERCUTIO
Could you not take some occasion without giving?   35

TYBALT
Mercutio, thou consortest with Romeo, —

MERCUTIO
Consort! What, dost thou make us minstrels? An thou make minstrels of us, look to hear nothing but discords. Here's my fiddlestick; here's that shall make you dance. Zounds, consort!

42: **reason coldly:** speak civilly (without passion)

47: **if he wear your livery:** i.e., if he is your servant

53: **appertaining:** appropriate

61: **tender:** value

BENVOLIO
>We talk here in the public haunt of men.   40
>Either withdraw unto some private place,
>Or reason coldly of your grievances,
>Or else depart. Here all eyes gaze on us.

MERCUTIO
>Men's eyes were made to look, and let them gaze.
>I will not budge for no man's pleasure, I.   45

[Enter ROMEO]

TYBALT
>Well, peace be with you, sir. Here comes my man.

MERCUTIO
>But I'll be hanged, sir, if he wear your livery.
>Marry, go before to field, he'll be your follower.
>Your worship in that sense may call him "man."

TYBALT
>Romeo, the hate I bear thee can afford   50
>No better term than this: thou art a villain.

ROMEO
>Tybalt, the reason that I have to love thee
>Doth much excuse the appertaining rage
>To such a greeting. Villain am I none;
>Therefore, farewell. I see thou knowest me not.   55

TYBALT
>Boy, this shall not excuse the injuries
>That thou hast done me; therefore, turn and draw.

ROMEO
>I do protest, I never injured thee,
>But love thee better than thou canst devise,
>Till thou shalt know the reason of my love.   60
>And so, good Capulet, which name I tender
>As dearly as my own, be satisfied.

64: **Alla stoccata:** a fencing thrust (Mercutio here is contemptuously referring to Tybalt, who is known as a skilled swordsman)

65–127:
Anton Lesser as Mercutio, Jasper Britton as Tybalt, Michael Sheen as Romeo
Ian Bannen as Mercutio, Nigel Davenport as Tybalt, Keith Michell as Romeo

tracks 11-12

65: **will you walk:** i.e., will you fight with me
67: **king of cats:** reference to Tybalt's name
68: **withal:** with
68: **dry-beat:** thrash
69: **pilcher:** scabbard (a very derogatory and insulting expression)
73: **passado:** in fencing, a motion forwards and thrust

Line 73: "Come, sir, your passado": The ensemble of The Shakespeare Theatre's 2001–2002 production directed by Rachael Kavanaugh
Photo: Carol Rosegg

77: **bandying:** fighting, contending
80: **I am sped:** i.e., my fate is decided
81: **nothing:** i.e., no wound

MERCUTIO
O calm, dishonourable, vile submission!
Alla stoccata carries it away.

[Draws]

Tybalt, you ratcatcher, will you walk? 65

TYBALT
What wouldst thou have with me?

MERCUTIO
Good king of cats, nothing but one of your nine lives that I mean
to make bold withal, and, as you shall use me hereafter, dry-beat
the rest of the eight. Will you pluck your sword out of his pilcher
by the ears? Make haste, lest mine be about your ears ere it be out. 70

TYBALT
I am for you.

[Drawing]

ROMEO
Gentle Mercutio, put thy rapier up.

MERCUTIO
Come, sir, your passado.

[They fight]

ROMEO
Draw, Benvolio. Beat down their weapons.
Gentlemen, for shame, forbear this outrage! 75
Tybalt, Mercutio, the prince expressly hath
Forbidden bandying in Verona streets.
Hold, Tybalt! Good Mercutio!
          [TYBALT stabs MERCUTIO and flies with his followers]

MERCUTIO
          I am hurt.
A plague o' both houses! I am sped. 80
Is he gone and hath nothing?

tracks 11-12

65–127:
Anton Lesser as Mercutio, Jasper Britton as Tybalt, Michael Sheen as Romeo
Ian Bannen as Mercutio, Nigel Davenport as Tybalt, Keith Michell as Romeo

88: **a grave man:** a pun: serious/dead (in the grave)

88: **I am peppered:** I am finished

91: **by the book of arithmetic:** strictly by the rules of fencing
(another reference to doing things "by the book")

96: **worms' meat:** food for worms

103: **effeminate:** cowardly

104: **temper:** disposition

104: **softened valour's steel:** tempered my bravery, weakened me

BENVOLIO
> What, art thou hurt?

MERCUTIO
> Ay, ay, a scratch, a scratch; marry, 'tis enough.
> Where is my page? Go, villain, fetch a surgeon.

[Exit Page]

ROMEO
> Courage, man, the hurt cannot be much.   85

MERCUTIO
> No, 'tis not so deep as a well, nor so wide as a church-door, but
> 'tis enough, 'twill serve. Ask for me tomorrow, and you shall find
> me a grave man. I am peppered, I warrant, for this world. A
> plague o' both your houses! Zounds, a dog, a rat, a mouse, a cat,
> to scratch a man to death! A braggart, a rogue, a villain, that   90
> fights by the book of arithmetic! Why the devil came you between
> us? I was hurt under your arm.

ROMEO
> I thought all for the best.

MERCUTIO
> Help me into some house, Benvolio,
> Or I shall faint. A plague o' both your houses!   95
> They have made worms' meat of me: I have it,
> And soundly too. Your houses!

[Exeunt MERCUTIO and BENVOLIO]

ROMEO
> This gentleman, the prince's near ally,
> My very friend, hath got his mortal hurt
> In my behalf. My reputation stained   100
> With Tybalt's slander; Tybalt, that an hour
> Hath been my cousin! O sweet Juliet,
> Thy beauty hath made me effeminate
> And in my temper softened valour's steel!

[Enter BENVOLIO]

tracks 11-12

65–127:
Anton Lesser as Mercutio, Jasper Britton as Tybalt, Michael Sheen as Romeo
Ian Bannen as Mercutio, Nigel Davenport as Tybalt, Keith Michell as Romeo

106: **aspired:** risen to

107: **scorn:** leave/depart

108: **doth depend:** shall continue

112: **respective lenity:** considerate gentleness or mercy

113: **conduct:** guide

Line 121: "This shall determine that": The ensemble of The Shakespeare Theatre's
1993–1994 production directed by Barry Kyle
Photo: Richard Anderson

123: **up:** stirring, agitated

BENVOLIO
  O Romeo, Romeo, brave Mercutio is dead.   105
  That gallant spirit hath aspired the clouds,
  Which too untimely here did scorn the earth.

ROMEO
  This day's black fate on more days doth depend;
  This but begins the woe others must end.

BENVOLIO
  Here comes the furious Tybalt back again.   110

ROMEO
  Alive, in triumph, and Mercutio slain!
  Away to heaven, respective lenity,
  And fire and fury be my conduct now!

                              [Enter TYBALT]

  Now, Tybalt, take the villain back again
  That late thou gavest me for Mercutio's soul   115
  Is but a little way above our heads,
  Staying for thine to keep him company.
  Either thou, or I, or both, must go with him.

TYBALT
  Thou, wretched boy, that didst consort him here,
  Shalt with him hence.   120

ROMEO
              This shall determine that.
                  [They fight. TYBALT falls]

BENVOLIO
  Romeo, away, be gone!
  The citizens are up, and Tybalt slain.
  Stand not amazed. The prince will doom thee death
  If thou art taken. Hence, be gone, away!   125

ROMEO
  O, I am fortune's fool!

65–127:
Anton Lesser as Mercutio, Jasper Britton as Tybalt, Michael Sheen as Romeo
Ian Bannen as Mercutio, Nigel Davenport as Tybalt, Keith Michell as Romeo

134: **discover:** tell

135: **manage:** course

145: **fair:** kindly, gently

145: **bethink:** to consider

BENVOLIO

          Why dost thou stay?

                                 [Exit ROMEO]
                              [Enter Citizens]

First Citizen
   Which way ran he that killed Mercutio?
   Tybalt, that murderer, which way ran he?

BENVOLIO
   There lies that Tybalt.   130

First Citizen
          Up, sir, go with me.
   I charge thee in the Prince's name, obey.
     [Enter PRINCE, old MONTAGUE, CAPULET, their Wives, and all]

PRINCE
   Where are the vile beginners of this fray?

BENVOLIO
   O noble Prince, I can discover all
   The unlucky manage of this fatal brawl.   135
   There lies the man, slain by young Romeo,
   That slew thy kinsman, brave Mercutio.

LADY CAPULET
   Tybalt, my cousin! O my brother's child!
   O prince! O cousin! Husband! O, the blood is spilt
   Of my dear kinsman! Prince, as thou art true,   140
   For blood of ours, shed blood of Montague.
   O cousin, cousin!

PRINCE
   Benvolio, who began this bloody fray?

BENVOLIO
   Tybalt, here slain, whom Romeo's hand did slay.
   Romeo, that spoke him fair, bid him bethink   145

146: **nice:** trivial

146: **withal:** at the same time

149: **spleen:** fire, impetuosity

152: **point to point:** sword to sword

156: **retorts it:** sends it back

160: **envious:** spiteful, malignant

161: **stout:** bold and resolute

J. P. Kemble deleted Benvolio's exposition of Romeo and Tybalt's fight.
Thus the audience learns of Romeo's punishment when Juliet does,
in her exchange with the Nurse in Act 3, Scene 2.

How nice the quarrel was, and urged withal
Your high displeasure. All this uttered
With gentle breath, calm look, knees humbly bowed,
Could not take truce with the unruly spleen
Of Tybalt, deaf to peace, but that he tilts   150
With piercing steel at bold Mercutio's breast,
Who all as hot, turns deadly point to point,
And, with a martial scorn, with one hand beats
Cold death aside, and with the other sends
It back to Tybalt, whose dexterity   155
Retorts it. Romeo, he cries aloud,
"Hold, friends! Friends, part!" and, swifter than his tongue,
His agile arm beats down their fatal points,
And 'twixt them rushes, underneath whose arm
An envious thrust from Tybalt hit the life   160
Of stout Mercutio, and then Tybalt fled.
But by and by comes back to Romeo,
Who had but newly entertained revenge,
And to 't they go like lightning, for, ere I
Could draw to part them, was stout Tybalt slain.   165
And, as he fell, did Romeo turn and fly.
This is the truth, or let Benvolio die.

LADY CAPULET
  He is a kinsman to the Montague.
  Affection makes him false; he speaks not true.
  Some twenty of them fought in this black strife,   170
  And all those twenty could but kill one life.
  I beg for justice, which thou, Prince, must give.
  Romeo slew Tybalt, Romeo must not live.

PRINCE
  Romeo slew him, he slew Mercutio;
  Who now the price of his dear blood doth owe?   175

MONTAGUE
  Not Romeo, Prince, he was Mercutio's friend.
  His fault concludes but what the law should end,
  The life of Tybalt.

182: **my blood:** my relatives, i.e., Mercutio

183: **amerce:** punish

J. P. Kemble's deletion of the scene between Benvolio and the Prince

PRINCE

And for that offense,
Immediately we do exile him hence.   180
I have an interest in your hate's proceeding,
My blood for your rude brawls doth lie a-bleeding.
But I'll amerce you with so strong a fine
That you shall all repent the loss of mine.
I will be deaf to pleading and excuses,   185
Nor tears nor prayers shall purchase out abuses.
Therefore use none. Let Romeo hence in haste,
Else, when he is found, that hour is his last.
Bear hence this body and attend our will.
Mercy but murders, pardoning those that kill.   190

[Exeunt]

1: **fiery-footed steeds:** horses of the sun god (According to Greek and Roman mythology, the sun is explained as the sun god driving a flaming chariot across the sky each day.)

2: **Phoebus:** another name for the Greek god Apollo, the sun-god

2: **waggoner:** charioteer

3: **Phaethon:** son of the sun-god and caretaker of the fire-horses

3: **to the west:** i.e., toward the sunset

5: **close:** obscuring

5: **love-performing night:** i.e., the time to make love

6: **wink:** shut or twinkle like the stars

12: **learn:** teach

12: **lose:** i.e., lose herself/her chastity

12: **winning match:** a fine husband

14: **hood:** conceal, cover to calm down agitation (another term from falconry)

14: **unmanned:** not accustomed to man (a term from falconry, also a pun meaning "virgin")

14: **bating:** beating the wings impatiently and fluttering away from the fist or perch (also a pun meaning "diminishing")

Act 3: Scene 2

JULIET
    Gallop apace, you fiery-footed steeds,
    Towards Phoebus' lodging. Such a waggoner
    As Phaethon would whip you to the west,
    And bring in cloudy night immediately.
    Spread thy close curtain, love-performing night,   5
    That runaway's eyes may wink and Romeo
    Leap to these arms, untalked of and unseen.
    Lovers can see to do their amorous rites
    By their own beauties; or, if love be blind,
    It best agrees with night. Come, civil night,   10
    Thou sober-suited matron, all in black,
    And learn me how to lose a winning match
    Played for a pair of stainless maidenhoods.
    Hood my unmanned blood, bating in my cheeks,
    With thy black mantle till strange love grow bold,   15
    Think true love acted simple modesty.
    Come, night. Come, Romeo. Come, thou day in night,
    For thou wilt lie upon the wings of night
    Whiter than new snow on a raven's back.
    Come, gentle night. Come, loving, black-browed night.   20
    Give me my Romeo, and, when he shall die,
    Take him and cut him out in little stars,
    And he will make the face of heaven so fine
    That all the world will be in love with night
    And pay no worship to the garish sun.   25
    O, I have bought the mansion of a love,
    But not possessed it, and though I am sold,
    Not yet enjoyed. So tedious is this day
    As is the night before some festival
    To an impatient child that hath new robes   30
    And may not wear them. O, here comes my Nurse,

Stage direction: **cords:** ropes, for the ladder

38: **weraday:** an exclamation of grief

48: **bare:** single, sole

48: **"I":** aye = yes

49: **cockatrice:** a mythical creature supposed to be produced from a cock's egg and to have so deadly an eye as to kill by its very look

50: **I am not..."I":** i.e., I am not myself if your answer is yes

53: **weal:** welfare, happiness

And she brings news; and every tongue that speaks
But Romeo's name speaks heavenly eloquence. —

[Enter NURSE, with cords]

Now, Nurse, what news? What hast thou there? The cords
That Romeo bid thee fetch?   35

NURSE

                    Ay, ay, the cords.

[Puts them down]

JULIET

Ay me! What news? Why dost thou wring thy hands?

NURSE

Ah, weraday, he's dead, he's dead, he's dead!
We are undone, lady, we are undone!
Alack the day! He's gone, he's killed, he's dead!   40

JULIET

Can heaven be so envious?

NURSE

                    Romeo can,
Though heaven cannot. O Romeo, Romeo!
Who ever would have thought it? Romeo!

JULIET

What devil art thou, that dost torment me thus?   45
This torture should be roared in dismal hell.
Hath Romeo slain himself? Say thou but "Ay,"
And that bare vowel "I" shall poison more
Than the death-darting eye of cockatrice.
I am not I, if there be such an "I,"   50
Or those eyes shut, that make thee answer "Ay."
If he be slain, say "Ay," or if not, "No."
Brief sounds determine my weal or woe.

NURSE

I saw the wound, I saw it with mine eyes —
God save the mark! — here on his manly breast.   55

56: **corse:** dead body

57: **bedaubed in:** soiled with

58: **swoundèd:** swooned

69: **dreadful trumpet...doom:** summoning to the last judgment, a bibilical reference to the trumpet which announces the apocalypse, or end of the world

76: **keep:** inhabit

79: **despisèd:** despicable

A piteous corse, a bloody piteous corse,
Pale, pale as ashes, all bedaubed in blood,
All in gore blood. I swoundèd at the sight.

JULIET
O, break, my heart, poor bankrupt, break at once!
To prison, eyes, ne'er look on liberty.   60
Vile earth, to earth resign; end motion here,
And thou and Romeo press one heavy bier!

NURSE
O Tybalt, Tybalt, the best friend I had!
O courteous Tybalt! Honest gentleman!
That ever I should live to see thee dead!   65

JULIET
What storm is this that blows so contrary?
Is Romeo slaughtered, and is Tybalt dead?
My dearest cousin and my dearer lord?
Then, dreadful trumpet, sound the general doom.
For who is living, if those two are gone?   70

NURSE
Tybalt is gone, and Romeo banishèd;
Romeo that killed him, he is banishèd.

JULIET
O God! Did Romeo's hand shed Tybalt's blood?

NURSE
It did, it did; alas the day, it did!

JULIET
O serpent heart, hid with a flow'ring face!   75
Did ever dragon keep so fair a cave?
Beautiful tyrant, fiend angelical!
Dove-feathered raven, wolvish-ravening lamb!
Despisèd substance of divinest show!
Just opposite to what thou justly seem'st,   80

83: **bower:** enclose

track 13

88–130:
Dame Judi Dench as the Nurse, Samantha Bond as Juliet

91: **aqua vitae:** strong drink

104: **wherefore:** why

107: **tributary:** paying tribute; also refers to rivers which branch off the central waterflow

A damnèd saint, an honourable villain!
O nature, what hadst thou to do in hell
When thou didst bower the spirit of a fiend
In mortal paradise of such sweet flesh?
Was ever book containing such vile matter   85
So fairly bound? O that deceit should dwell
In such a gorgeous palace!

NURSE
    There's no trust,
No faith, no honesty in men; all perjured,
All forsworn, all naught, all dissemblers.   90
Ah, where's my man? Give me some aqua vitae.
These griefs, these woes, these sorrows make me old.
Shame come to Romeo!

JULIET
    Blistered be thy tongue
For such a wish! He was not born to shame.   95
Upon his brow shame is ashamed to sit,
For 'tis a throne where honour may be crowned
Sole monarch of the universal earth.
O, what a beast was I to chide at him!

NURSE
Will you speak well of him that killed your cousin?   100

JULIET
Shall I speak ill of him that is my husband?
Ah, poor my lord, what tongue shall smooth thy name,
When I, thy three-hours wife, have mangled it?
But wherefore, villain, didst thou kill my cousin?
That villain cousin would have killed my husband.   105
Back, foolish tears, back to your native spring.
Your tributary drops belong to woe,
Which you, mistaking, offer up to joy.
My husband lives, that Tybalt would have slain,
And Tybalt's dead, that would have slain my husband.   110
All this is comfort; wherefore weep I then?
Some word there was, worser than Tybalt's death,
That murdered me. I would forget it fain;

track 13

88–130:
Dame Judi Dench as the Nurse, Samantha Bond as Juliet

113: **fain:** gladly, willingly

124: **modern:** commonplace

125: **rearward:** the last troop, rearguard (in this case suggesting a following attack)

136: **beguiled:** tricked

139: **maiden-widowèd:** having become a widow while still a virgin

143: **wot:** know

But, O, it presses to my memory,
Like damnèd guilty deeds to sinners' minds.   115
"Tybalt is dead, and Romeo banishèd."
That "banishèd," that one word "banishèd"
Hath slain ten thousand Tybalts. Tybalt's death
Was woe enough if it had ended there.
Or, if sour woe delights in fellowship   120
And needly will be ranked with other griefs,
Why followed not, when she said, "Tybalt's dead,"
"Thy father," or "thy mother," nay, or both,
Which modern lamentation might have moved?
But with a rearward following Tybalt's death,   125
"Romeo is banished." To speak that word,
Is father, mother, Tybalt, Romeo, Juliet,
All slain, all dead. "Romeo is banishèd!"
There is no end, no limit, measure, bound,
In that word's death. No words can that woe sound.   130
Where is my father and my mother, nurse?

NURSE
Weeping and wailing over Tybalt's corse.
Will you go to them? I will bring you thither.

JULIET
Wash they his wounds with tears? Mine shall be spent,
When theirs are dry, for Romeo's banishment.   135
Take up those cords. Poor ropes, you are beguiled,
Both you and I, for Romeo is exiled.
He made you for a highway to my bed,
But I, a maid, die maiden-widowèd.
Come, cords, come, Nurse. I'll to my wedding bed,   140
And death, not Romeo, take my maidenhead!

NURSE
Hie to your chamber. I'll find Romeo
To comfort you; I wot well where he is.
Hark ye, your Romeo will be here at night.
I'll to him; he is hid at Laurence' cell.   145
JULIET
O, find him! Give this ring to my true knight,
And bid him come to take his last farewell.

                                                      [*Exeunt*]

2: **Affliction...parts:** bad luck is attached to him in every way

4: **doom:** sentence, judgment

8: **sour company:** i.e., sorrow

11: **vanished:** arose, like vapor

14: **hath more terror in his look:** is more terrifying

Act 3: Scene 3

[Enter FRIAR LAURENCE]

FRIAR LAURENCE
Romeo, come forth; come forth, thou fearful man.
Affliction is enamoured of thy parts,
And thou art wedded to calamity.

[Enter ROMEO]

ROMEO
Father, what news? What is the Prince's doom?
What sorrow craves acquaintance at my hand   5
That I yet know not?

FRIAR LAURENCE
                    Too familiar
Is my dear son with such sour company.
I bring thee tidings of the Prince's doom.

ROMEO
What less than doomsday is the Prince's doom?   10

FRIAR LAURENCE
A gentler judgment vanished from his lips,
Not body's death, but body's banishment.

ROMEO
Ha, banishment? Be merciful, say "death,"
For exile hath more terror in his look,
Much more than death. Do not say "banishment."   15

FRIAR LAURENCE
Hence from Verona art thou banishèd.
Be patient, for the world is broad and wide.

18: **without:** beyond

Line 18: "There is no world without Verona walls": Joseph Marcell as Friar Lawrence and Paul Whitthorne as Romeo in The Shakespeare Theatre's 2001–2002 production directed by Rachael Kavanaugh
Photo: Carol Rosegg

track 14

18–77:
Kenneth Branagh as Romeo, Sir John Gielgud as Friar Laurence

20: **hence, banishèd:** Banished from this place

22: **mistermed:** called by the wrong name

26: **Thy fault...death:** Your crime is punishable by death

27: **rushed aside:** circumvented

34: **validity:** value

39: **vestal:** virginal

49: **attend:** accompany

ROMEO

 There is no world without Verona walls
 But purgatory, torture, hell itself.
 Hence, banishèd is banished from the world,   20
 And world's exile is death. Then banishèd
 Is death mistermed. Calling death "banishèd,"
 Thou cutt'st my head off with a golden axe
 And smilest upon the stroke that murders me.

FRIAR LAURENCE

 O deadly sin, O rude unthankfulness!   25
 Thy fault our law calls death, but the kind Prince,
 Taking thy part, hath rushed aside the law,
 And turned that black word "death" to "banishment."
 This is dear mercy, and thou seest it not.

ROMEO

 'Tis torture and not mercy. Heaven is here,   30
 Where Juliet lives, and every cat and dog
 And little mouse, every unworthy thing,
 Live here in heaven and may look on her,
 But Romeo may not. More validity,
 More honourable state, more courtship lives   35
 In carrion-flies than Romeo. They may seize
 On the white wonder of dear Juliet's hand
 And steal immortal blessing from her lips,
 Who even in pure and vestal modesty
 Still blush, as thinking their own kisses sin.   40
 But Romeo may not; he is banishèd.
 Flies may do this, but I from this must fly.
 They are free men, but I am banishèd.
 And say'st thou yet that exile is not death?
 Hadst thou no poison mixed, no sharp-ground knife,   45
 No sudden mean of death, though ne'er so mean,
 But "banishèd" to kill me? "Banishèd?"
 O friar, the damnèd use that word in hell.
 Howling attends it. How hast thou the heart,
 Being a divine, a ghostly confessor,   50
 A sin absolver, and my friend professed,
 To mangle me with that word "banishèd?"

track 14

18–77:
Kenneth Branagh as Romeo, Sir John Gielgud as Friar Laurence

53: **fond:** foolish, silly

56: **Adversity...philosophy:** i.e., philosophy makes adversity sweet

60: **displant:** transplant

71: **Taking the measure...grave:** measuring the ground to prepare a grave
(i.e., in anticipation of his death)

FRIAR LAURENCE
Thou fond mad man, hear me a little speak.

ROMEO
O, thou wilt speak again of banishment.

FRIAR LAURENCE
I'll give thee armour to keep off that word:,   55
Adversity's sweet milk, philosophy,
To comfort thee, though thou art banishèd.

ROMEO
Yet "banishèd?" Hang up philosophy!
Unless philosophy can make a Juliet,
Displant a town, reverse a Prince's doom,   60
It helps not, it prevails not. Talk no more.

FRIAR LAURENCE
O, then I see that madmen have no ears.

ROMEO
How should they, when that wise men have no eyes?

FRIAR LAURENCE
Let me dispute with thee of thy estate.

ROMEO
Thou canst not speak of that thou dost not feel.   65
Wert thou as young as I, Juliet thy love,
An hour but married, Tybalt murdered,
Doting like me and like me banishèd,
Then mightst thou speak, then mightst thou tear thy hair
And fall upon the ground, as I do now,   70
Taking the measure of an unmade grave.

[*Knocking within*]

FRIAR LAURENCE
Arise! One knocks. Good Romeo, hide thyself.

track 14

18–77:
Kenneth Branagh as Romeo, Sir John Gielgud as Friar Laurence

74: **infold:** enclose, wrap

78: **simpleness:** silliness

86: **he is even in my mistress' case:** he is in the same situation as my mistress

90: **and:** if

92: **so deep an O:** piteous moans expressing great pain

ROMEO
    Not I, unless the breath of heartsick groans,
    Mist-like, infold me from the search of eyes.

                                                            [Knocking]

FRIAR LAURENCE
    Hark, how they knock! — Who's there? — Romeo, arise.   75
    Thou wilt be taken. — Stay awhile. — Stand up.

                                                            [Knocking]

    Run to my study. — By and by! — God's will,
    What simpleness is this! — I come, I come!

                                                            [Knocking]

    Who knocks so hard? Whence come you? What's your will?

NURSE
                                                      [Within]
    Let me come in, and you shall know my errand.   80
    I come from Lady Juliet.

FRIAR LAURENCE
                  Welcome then.

                                                    [Enter NURSE]

NURSE
    O holy friar, O, tell me, holy friar,
    Where's my lady's lord? Where's Romeo?

FRIAR LAURENCE
    There on the ground, with his own tears made drunk.   85

NURSE
    O, he is even in my mistress' case,
    Just in her case! O woeful sympathy!
    Piteous predicament! Even so lies she,
    Blubb'ring and weeping, weeping and blubb'ring.
    Stand up, stand up; stand, and you be a man.   90
    For Juliet's sake, for her sake, rise and stand.
    Why should you fall into so deep an O?

95: **spakest:** did you speak (archaic past verb tense)

98: **blood removed but little:** i.e., a close relative

100: **my concealed lady:** Juliet, his secret wife

100: **cancelled:** annulled

track 15

108–165:
Sir John Gielgud as Friar Laurence, Kenneth Branagh as Romeo,
Dame Judi Dench as the Nurse

110: **sack:** destroy and pillage

112: **hold:** stop

116: **unseemly woman in a seeming man:** inappropriately womanish behavior
while appearing to be a man

117: **ill-beseeming:** unnatural

ROMEO
  Nurse!

NURSE
  Ah sir, ah sir, death's the end of all.

ROMEO
  Spakest thou of Juliet? How is it with her?   95
  Doth not she think me an old murderer,
  Now I have stained the childhood of our joy
  With blood removed but little from her own?
  Where is she? And how doth she? And what says
  My concealed lady to our cancelled love?   100

NURSE
  O, she says nothing, sir, but weeps and weeps,
  And now falls on her bed, and then starts up,
  And Tybalt calls, and then on Romeo cries,
  And then down falls again.

ROMEO
                    As if that name,   105
  Shot from the deadly level of a gun,
  Did murder her, as that name's cursed hand
  Murdered her kinsman. O, tell me, friar, tell me,
  In what vile part of this anatomy
  Doth my name lodge? Tell me, that I may sack   110
  The hateful mansion.

                                            [*Drawing his sword*]

FRIAR LAURENCE
                    Hold thy desperate hand!
  Art thou a man? Thy form cries out thou art.
  Thy tears are womanish. Thy wild acts denote
  The unreasonable fury of a beast.   115
  Unseemly woman in a seeming man,
  And ill-beseeming beast in seeming both!
  Thou hast amazed me. By my holy order,
  I thought thy disposition better tempered.

108–165:
*Sir John Gielgud as Friar Laurence, Kenneth Branagh as Romeo,
Dame Judi Dench as the Nurse*

track 15

123: **rail'st:** scold

127: **usurer:** one who lends money and takes interest for it, which was thought disreputable at that time

129: **bedeck:** adorn, grace

132: **dear love...perjury:** i.e., the love he has sworn is false

136: **powder:** gunpowder

136: **flask:** powder horn, usually made of the horn of an ox or cow, and used for carrying gunpowder

138: **dismembered...defence:** i.e., blown up with your own gunpowder

140: **but lately dead:** all but dead

141: **happy:** lucky, fortunate

152: **watch be set:** the guards are in position

155: **blaze:** announce

Hast thou slain Tybalt? Wilt thou slay thyself? 120
And slay thy lady that in thy life lies
By doing damnèd hate upon thyself?
Why rail'st thou on thy birth? The heaven and earth?
Since birth and heaven and earth, all three do meet
In thee at once, which thou at once wouldst lose? 125
Fie, fie, thou shamest thy shape, thy love, thy wit,
Which, like a usurer, abound'st in all,
And usest none in that true use indeed,
Which should bedeck thy shape, thy love, thy wit.
Thy noble shape is but a form of wax, 130
Digressing from the valour of a man.
Thy dear love sworn but hollow perjury,
Killing that love which thou hast vowed to cherish.
Thy wit, that ornament to shape and love,
Misshapen in the conduct of them both, 135
Like powder in a skilless soldier's flask,
Is set afire by thine own ignorance,
And thou dismembered with thine own defence.
What, rouse thee, man! Thy Juliet is alive,
For whose dear sake thou wast but lately dead. 140
There art thou happy. Tybalt would kill thee,
But thou slewest Tybalt. There are thou happy too.
The law that threatened death becomes thy friend
And turns it to exile. There art thou happy.
A pack of blessings light up upon thy back. 145
Happiness courts thee in her best array,
But, like a misbehaved and sullen wench,
Thou pouts upon thy fortune and thy love.
Take heed, take heed, for such die miserable.
Go, get thee to thy love, as was decreed. 150
Ascend her chamber hence and comfort her.
But look thou stay not till the watch be set,
For then thou canst not pass to Mantua,
Where thou shalt live, till we can find a time
To blaze your marriage, reconcile your friends, 155
Beg pardon of the Prince, and call thee back
With twenty hundred thousand times more joy
Than thou went'st forth in lamentation.

track 15

108–165:
Sir John Gielgud as Friar Laurence, Kenneth Branagh as Romeo,
Dame Judi Dench as the Nurse

168: **hie you:** hurry

170: **here stands all your state:** these are your choices

174: **signify:** make you aware

175: **every good hap...here:** every piece of good news that happens

177: **past:** beyond, exceeding

Go before, nurse. Commend me to thy lady,
And bid her hasten all the house to bed, 160
Which heavy sorrow makes them apt unto.
Romeo is coming.

NURSE
O Lord, I could have stayed here all the night
To hear good counsel. O, what learning is!
My lord, I'll tell my lady you will come. 165

ROMEO
Do so, and bid my sweet prepare to chide.

NURSE
Here, sir, a ring she bid me give you, sir.
Hie you, make haste, for it grows very late.

[Exit]

ROMEO
How well my comfort is revived by this!

FRIAR LAURENCE
Go hence; good night; and here stands all your state. 170
Either be gone before the watch be set,
Or by the break of day disguised from hence,
Sojourn in Mantua. I'll find out your man,
And he shall signify from time to time
Every good hap to you that chances here. 175
Give me thy hand. 'Tis late. Farewell, good night.

ROMEO
But that a joy past joy calls out on me,
It were a grief, so brief to part with thee.
Farewell.

[Exeunt]

2: **move:** persuade

11: **mewed up to her heaviness:** shut up in her grief (*mew* is a term from falconry; it is the place in which the hawk is cooped up when it molts)

12: **desperate tender:** reckless or risky offer (reckless because it is made without consulting Juliet first)

15: **ere:** before

17: **mark you me:** pay attention/listen to me

Act 3: Scene 4

[*Enter old CAPULET, his wife, and PARIS*]

CAPULET
 Things have fall'n out, sir, so unluckily,
 That we have had no time to move our daughter.
 Look you, she loved her kinsman Tybalt dearly,
 And so did I. — Well, we were born to die.
 'Tis very late, she'll not come down tonight.   5
 I promise you, but for your company,
 I would have been abed an hour ago.

PARIS
 These times of woe afford no times to woo.
 Madam, good night. Commend me to your daughter.

LADY CAPULET
 I will, and know her mind early tomorrow.   10
 Tonight she is mewed up to her heaviness.

CAPULET
 Sir Paris, I will make a desperate tender
 Of my child's love. I think she will be ruled
 In all respects by me; nay, more, I doubt it not. —
 Wife, go you to her ere you go to bed.   15
 Acquaint her here of my son Paris' love;
 And bid her, mark you me, on Wednesday next —
 But, soft! What day is this?

PARIS
                    Monday, my lord,

CAPULET
 Monday, ha, ha! Well, Wednesday is too soon.   20
 O' Thursday let it be. O' Thursday, tell her

ROMEO & JULIET [214

24: **keep no great ado:** keep it simple

26: **carelessly:** in low esteem

33: **against:** for

34: **light to my chamber:** guide me to my chamber with light

35: **Afore me!:** A mild oath (by my soul!)

She shall be married to this noble earl.
Will you be ready? Do you like this haste?
We'll keep no great ado, a friend or two.
For, hark you, Tybalt being slain so late,   25
It may be thought we held him carelessly,
Being our kinsman, if we revel much.
Therefore we'll have some half a dozen friends,
And there an end. But what say you to Thursday?

PARIS

My lord, I would that Thursday were tomorrow.   30

CAPULET

Well get you gone. O' Thursday be it, then.
Go you to Juliet ere you go to bed.
Prepare her, wife, against this wedding day.
Farewell, my lord. — Light to my chamber, ho!
Afore me! — It is so very very late   35
That we may call it early by and by.
Good night.

                                              [*Exeunt*]

1–36:
Kate Beckinsale as Juliet, Michael Sheen as Romeo
Claire Bloom as Juliet, Albert Finney as Romeo

Line 1: "Wilt thou be gone?": Julia Marlowe as Juliet and E. H. Sothern as Romeo (1904)
Folger Shakespeare Library

2: the nightingale...the lark: The nightingale usually sings in the evening, signifying the onset of night, while the lark usually sings in the morning, indicating the breaking of day

7: envious streaks: i.e., the dawn (envious because it intrudes on their intimacy)

9: jocund: lively, brisk

13: meteor that the sun exhale: meteors were thought to originate in the sun and represented a bad omen

20: reflex of Cynthia's brow: the moon's reflection (Cynthia = goddess of the moon)

22: vaulty: arched, concave

Act 3: Scene 5

[*Enter ROMEO and JULIET aloft*]

JULIET
  Wilt thou be gone? It is not yet near day:
  It was the nightingale, and not the lark,
  That pierced the fearful hollow of thine ear.
  Nightly she sings on yon pomegranate tree.
  Believe me, love, it was the nightingale.   5

ROMEO
  It was the lark, the herald of the morn,
  No nightingale. Look, love, what envious streaks
  Do lace the severing clouds in yonder east.
  Night's candles are burnt out, and jocund day
  Stands tiptoe on the misty mountain tops.   10
  I must be gone and live, or stay and die.

JULIET
  Yond light is not daylight, I know it, I.
  It is some meteor that the sun exhale,
  To be to thee this night a torchbearer,
  And light thee on thy way to Mantua.   15
  Therefore stay yet. Thou need'st not to be gone.

ROMEO
  Let me be ta'en, let me be put to death;
  I am content, so thou wilt have it so.
  I'll say yon grey is not the morning's eye;
  'tis but the pale reflex of Cynthia's brow.   20
  Nor that is not the lark, whose notes do beat
  The vaulty heaven so high above our heads.
  I have more care to stay than will to go.
  Come, death, and welcome! Juliet wills it so.
  How is't, my soul? Let's talk; it is not day.   25

1–36:
Kate Beckinsale as Juliet, Michael Sheen as Romeo
Claire Bloom as Juliet, Albert Finney as Romeo

28: **discords:** loud, bad sounds (a pun on chaos)

29: **division:** musical variations

33: **affray:** frighten

34: **hunt's-up:** a hunting reveille, a rousing hunting tune played in the morning

Line 36: "More light and light, more dark and dark our woes!": Paul Whitthorne as Romeo and Jennifer Ikeda as Juliet in The Shakespeare Theatre's 2001–2002 production, directed by Rachael Kavanaugh
Photo: Carol Rosegg

JULIET
  It is, it is. Hie hence, be gone, away!
  It is the lark that sings so out of tune,
  Straining harsh discords and unpleasing sharps.
  Some say the lark makes sweet division;
  This doth not so, for she divideth us.   30
  Some say the lark and loathed toad change eyes.
  O, now I would they had changed voices too.
  Since arm from arm that voice doth us affray,
  Hunting thee hence with hunt's-up to the day,
  O, now be gone. More light and light it grows.   35

ROMEO
  More light and light, more dark and dark our woes!

                                        [Enter NURSE]

NURSE
  Madam.

JULIET
  Nurse?

NURSE
  Your lady mother is coming to your chamber.
  The day is broke; be wary, look about.   40
                                     [Exit]

JULIET
  Then, window, let day in, and let life out.

ROMEO
  Farewell, farewell! One kiss, and I'll descend.

                                   [Romeo descends]

JULIET
  Art thou gone so? Love, lord, ay, husband, friend!
  I must hear from thee every day in the hour,
  For in a minute there are many days.   45
  O, by this count I shall be much in years
  Ere I again behold my Romeo!

Susan Shentall as Juliet and Laurence Harvey as Romeo in Renato Castellani's 1954
movie production
Courtesy: Douglas Lanier

54: **ill-divining:** foretelling evil

59: **dry:** thirsty

68: **unaccustomed:** unusual

68: **procures:** brings

ROMEO
    Farewell!
    I will omit no opportunity
    That may convey my greetings, love, to thee.   50

JULIET
    O think'st thou we shall ever meet again?

ROMEO
    I doubt it not, and all these woes shall serve
    For sweet discourses in our time to come.

JULIET
    O God, I have an ill-divining soul.
    Methinks I see thee now, thou art so low,   55
    As one dead in the bottom of a tomb.
    Either my eyesight fails, or thou look'st pale.

ROMEO
    And trust me, love, in my eye so do you.
    Dry sorrow drinks our blood. Adieu, adieu!

                                                      [Exit]

JULIET
    O fortune, fortune! All men call thee fickle.   60
    If thou art fickle, what dost thou with him
    That is renowned for faith? Be fickle, fortune,
    For then, I hope, thou wilt not keep him long,
    But send him back.

LADY CAPULET
                                        [Within]
    Ho, daughter! Are you up?   65

JULIET
    Who is't that calls? Is it my lady mother?
    Is she not down so late, or up so early?
    What unaccustomed cause procures her hither?
                                    [Enter LADY CAPULET]

71: **evermore:** all the time

75: **much of grief...want of wit:** i.e., excessive grief is a sign of diminished mental faculties

76: **feeling:** deeply felt

85: **asunder:** parted

LADY CAPULET
  Why, how now, Juliet?

JULIET
                    Madam, I am not well.   70

LADY CAPULET
  Evermore weeping for your cousin's death?
  What, wilt thou wash him from his grave with tears?
  An if thou couldst, thou couldst not make him live.
  Therefore, have done. Some grief shows much of love,
  But much of grief shows still some want of wit.   75

JULIET
  Yet let me weep for such a feeling loss.

LADY CAPULET
  So shall you feel the loss, but not the friend
  Which you weep for.

JULIET
                    Feeling so the loss,
  Cannot choose but ever weep the friend.   80

LADY CAPULET
  Well, girl, thou weep'st not so much for his death,
  As that the villain lives which slaughtered him.

JULIET
  What villain, madam?

LADY CAPULET
                    That same villain, Romeo.

JULIET
  [*Aside*] Villain and he be many miles asunder. —   85
  God pardon him! I do, with all my heart,
  And yet no man like he doth grieve my heart.

90: **venge:** avenge

93: **runagate:** vagabond

94: **unaccustomed dram:** deadly potion

98: **—dead—** : (note that the break allows her mother to think she means "till I behold him dead," but she is really suggesting "dead is my poor heart")

101: **temper:** mix, administer, or dilute so as to weaken

105: **wreak:** revenge, let loose

111: **careful:** attentive, provident

112: **heaviness:** sorrow

LADY CAPULET
    That is because the traitor murderer lives.

JULIET
    Ay, madam, from the reach of these my hands,
    Would none but I might venge my cousin's death.   90

LADY CAPULET
    We will have vengeance for it, fear thou not,
    Then weep no more. I'll send to one in Mantua
    Where that same banished runagate doth live,
    Shall give him such an unaccustomed dram,
    That he shall soon keep Tybalt company.   95
    And then, I hope, thou wilt be satisfied.

JULIET
    Indeed, I never shall be satisfied
    With Romeo, till I behold him — dead —
    Is my poor heart for a kinsman vexed.
    Madam, if you could find out but a man   100
    To bear a poison, I would temper it,
    That Romeo should, upon receipt thereof,
    Soon sleep in quiet. O, how my heart abhors
    To hear him named and cannot come to him
    To wreak the love I bore my cousin   105
    Upon his body that slaughtered him!

LADY CAPULET
    Find thou the means, and I'll find such a man.
    But now I'll tell thee joyful tidings, girl.

JULIET
    And joy comes well in such a needy time.
    What are they, I beseech your ladyship?   110

LADY CAPULET
    Well, well, thou hast a careful father, child,
    One who, to put thee from thy heaviness,
    Hath sorted out a sudden day of joy
    That thou expects not nor I looked not for.

133: **conduit:** a human figurine spouting water (as on a fountain)

134: **showering:** crying

135: **counterfeit'st:** imitates, resembles

135: **bark:** ship

141: **tempest-tossed:** tossed or thrown about by a tempest or a storm

142: **decree:** decision

JULIET
  Madam, in happy time, what day is that?   115

LADY CAPULET
  Marry, my child, early next Thursday morn,
  The gallant, young and noble gentleman,
  The County Paris, at Saint Peter's Church
  Shall happily make thee there a joyful bride.

JULIET
  Now, by Saint Peter's Church and Peter too,   120
  He shall not make me there a joyful bride.
  I wonder at this haste that I must wed,
  Ere he, that should be husband, comes to woo.
  I pray you, tell my lord and father, madam,
  I will not marry yet; and, when I do, I swear,   125
  It shall be Romeo, whom you know I hate,
  Rather than Paris. These are news indeed!

LADY CAPULET
  Here comes your father. Tell him so yourself,
  And see how he will take it at your hands.

                    [*Enter CAPULET and NURSE*]

CAPULET
  When the sun sets, the air doth drizzle dew,   130
  But for the sunset of my brother's son
  It rains downright.
  How now! A conduit, girl? What, still in tears?
  Evermore showering? In one little body
  Thou counterfeit'st a bark, a sea, a wind.   135
  For still thy eyes, which I may call the sea,
  Do ebb and flow with tears; the bark thy body is,
  Sailing in this salt flood; the winds, thy sighs;
  Who, raging with thy tears and they with them,
  Without a sudden calm, will overset   140
  Thy tempest-tossed body. How now, wife!
  Have you delivered to her our decree?

145: **take me with you:** explain it more clearly (i.e., I do not follow your meaning)

153: **chop-logic:** plausible but fallacious argument

155: **minion:** pert and saucy person

157: **fettle:** prepare

159: **hurdle:** sleigh on which criminals are drawn to the place of execution

160: **green-sickness:** a kind of anemia (chlorosis) affecting young women

160: **baggage:** term of contempt for a worthless woman

161: **tallow-face:** pale (like wax) creature

LADY CAPULET
    Ay, sir, but she will none; she gives you thanks.
    I would the fool were married to her grave!

CAPULET
    Soft, take me with you, take me with you, wife.   145
    How? Will she none? Doth she not give us thanks?
    Is she not proud? Doth she not count her blest,
    Unworthy as she is, that we have wrought
    So worthy a gentleman to be her bride?

JULIET
    Not proud, you have, but thankful, that you have.   150
    Proud can I never be of what I hate,
    But thankful even for hate that is meant love.

CAPULET
    How now, how now, chop-logic! What is this?
    "Proud," and "I thank you," and "I thank you not,"
    And yet "not proud?" Mistress minion, you,   155
    Thank me no thankings, nor, proud me no prouds,
    But fettle your fine joints 'gainst Thursday next,
    To go with Paris to Saint Peter's Church,
    Or I will drag thee on a hurdle thither.
    Out, you green-sickness carrion! Out, you baggage!   160
    You tallow-face!

LADY CAPULET
                Fie, fie! What, are you mad?

JULIET
    Good father, I beseech you on my knees,
    Hear me with patience but to speak a word.

CAPULET
    Hang thee, young baggage! Disobedient wretch!   165
    I tell thee what: get thee to church o' Thursday,
    Or never after look me in the face.
    Speak not, reply not, do not answer me;

169: **My fingers itch:** i.e., He wants to beat her

Line 171: "But now I see this one is one too much": Jennifer Ikeda as Juliet and Edward Gero as Capulet in The Shakespeare Theatre's 2001–2002 production, directed by Rachael Kavanaugh
Photo: Carol Rosegg

173: **hilding:** menial wretch

175: **rate:** berate, yell at

177: **good prudence:** (used as an expletive)

177: **smatter:** chatter

179: **god-den:** good evening (spoken in reproof)

185: **God's bread:** an expletive

187: **care:** concern

190: **demesnes:** estates

My fingers itch. — Wife, we scarce thought us blest
That God had lent us but this only child,   170
But now I see this one is one too much
And that we have a curse in having her. —
Out on her, hilding!

NURSE
                    God in heaven bless her!
You are to blame, my lord, to rate her so.   175

CAPULET
    And why, my lady wisdom? Hold your tongue.
    Good prudence, smatter with your gossips, go.

NURSE
    I speak no treason.

CAPULET
                    O, God ye god-den.

NURSE
    May not one speak?   180

CAPULET
                    Peace, you mumbling fool!
    Utter your gravity o'er a gossip's bowl,
    For here we need it not.

LADY CAPULET
                    You are too hot.

CAPULET
    God's bread! it makes me mad: 185
    Day, night, hour, tide, time, work, play,
    Alone, in company, still my care hath been
    To have her matched. And having now provided
    A gentleman of noble parentage,
    Of fair demesnes, youthful, and nobly lined,   190
    Stuffed, as they say, with honourable parts,

193: **puling:** whining

194: **mammet:** puppet, doll

196: **pardon:** 1) forgive and 2) give permission to leave the house (permanently)

200: **advise:** consider

201: **an:** if

205: **bethink you:** seriously consider it

205: **I'll not be forsworn:** I will keep my word

219: **stratagems:** tests, warlike maneuvers

Proportioned as one's thought would wish a man.
And then to have a wretched puling fool,
A whining mammet, in her fortune's tender,
To answer "I'll not wed; I cannot love;   195
I am too young; I pray you, pardon me."
But, an you will not wed, I'll pardon you.
Graze where you will you shall not house with me.
Look to't, think on't, I do not use to jest.
Thursday is near. Lay hand on heart; advise.   200
An you be mine, I'll give you to my friend.
And you be not, hang, beg, starve, die in the streets,
For by my soul, I'll ne'er acknowledge thee,
Nor what is mine shall never do thee good.
Trust to't; bethink you; I'll not be forsworn.   205
                                                                    [*Exit*]

JULIET
  Is there no pity sitting in the clouds
  That sees into the bottom of my grief?
  O, sweet my mother, cast me not away.
  Delay this marriage for a month, a week,
  Or, if you do not, make the bridal bed   210
  In that dim monument where Tybalt lies.

LADY CAPULET
  Talk not to me, for I'll not speak a word.
  Do as thou wilt, for I have done with thee.

                                                                    [*Exit*]

JULIET
  O God! — O Nurse, how shall this be prevented?
  My husband is on earth, my faith in heaven.   215
  How shall that faith return again to earth,
  Unless that husband send it me from heaven
  By leaving earth? Comfort me, counsel me.
  Alack, alack, that heaven should practise stratagems
  Upon so soft a subject as myself.   220
  What say'st thou? hast thou not a word of joy?
  Some comfort, Nurse.

225: **challenge you:** i.e., claim you for his wife

230: **dishclout:** dishcloth

232: **beshrew:** my oath (i.e., woe to)

233: **happy:** fortunate

240: **Amen:** This response from Juliet changes the Nurse's previous line into a prayer instead of a mild oath; however, the Nurse does not pick up on this.

NURSE
                    Faith, here it is.
Romeo is banished and all the world to nothing
That he dares ne'er come back to challenge you,   225
Or, if he do, it needs must be by stealth.
Then, since the case so stands as now it doth,
I think it best you married with the County.
O, he's a lovely gentleman.
Romeo's a dishclout to him. An eagle, madam,   230
Hath not so green, so quick, so fair an eye
As Paris hath. Beshrew my very heart,
I think you are happy in this second match,
For it excels your first, or if it did not,
Your first is dead, or 'twere as good he were   235
As living here and you no use of him.

JULIET
Speak'st thou from thy heart?

NURSE
                    And from my soul too,
Else beshrew them both.

JULIET
                    Amen.   240

NURSE
                    What?

JULIET
Well, thou hast comforted me marvellous much.
Go in, and tell my lady I am gone,
Having displeased my father, to Laurence' cell,
To make confession and to be absolved.   245

NURSE
Marry, I will, and this is wisely done.

                                        [*Exit*]

247: **Ancient damnation:** Juliet is cursing the Nurse

248: **wish me thus forsworn:** have me break my marriage vows

252: **bosom:** i.e., my heart

252: **twain:** parted, separated

JULIET
    Ancient damnation! O most wicked fiend!
    Is it more sin to wish me thus forsworn,
    Or to dispraise my lord with that same tongue
    Which she hath praised him with above compare   250
    So many thousand times? Go, counsellor;
    Thou and my bosom henceforth shall be twain.
    I'll to the friar to know his remedy.
    If all else fail, myself have power to die.

                                      [Exit]

[Romeo and Juliet

Act 4

3: **I...slack his haste:** i.e., I won't slow him down by hesitating

6: **immoderately:** excessively

8: **Venus:** goddess of beauty and love

13: **minded:** in her thoughts

13: **by herself alone:** i.e., when she is by herself

14: **May be...by society:** i.e., social interaction will make her forget

Act 4: Scene 1]

[*Enter FRIAR LAURENCE and COUNTY PARIS*]

FRIAR LAURENCE
On Thursday, sir? The time is very short.

PARIS
My father Capulet will have it so,
And I am nothing slow to slack his haste.

FRIAR LAURENCE
You say you do not know the lady's mind?
Uneven is the course; I like it not.   5

PARIS
Immoderately she weeps for Tybalt's death,
And therefore have I little talked of love,
For Venus smiles not in a house of tears.
Now, sir, her father counts it dangerous
That she doth give her sorrow so much sway,   10
And in his wisdom hastes our marriage,
To stop the inundation of her tears
Which, too much minded by herself alone,
May be put from her by society.
Now do you know the reason of this haste.   15

FRIAR LAURENCE
[*Aside*] I would I knew not why it should be slowed. —
Look, sir, here comes the lady towards my cell.

[*Enter JULIET*]

PARIS
Happily met, my lady and my wife!

22: **certain:** truthful, definite

32: **it:** i.e., her face

32: **their spite:** i.e., her tears' spiteful attack

33: **with that report:** with those words

JULIET
   That may be, sir, when I may be a wife.

PARIS
   That may be must be, love, on Thursday next.   20

JULIET
   What must be shall be.

FRIAR LAURENCE
               That's a certain text.

PARIS
   Come you to make confession to this father?

JULIET
   To answer that, I should confess to you.

PARIS
   Do not deny to him that you love me.   25

JULIET
   I will confess to you that I love him.

PARIS
   So will ye, I am sure, that you love me.

JULIET
   If I do so, it will be of more price
   Being spoke behind your back than to your face.

PARIS
   Poor soul, thy face is much abused with tears.   30

JULIET
   The tears have got small victory by that,
   For it was bad enough before their spite.

PARIS
   Thou wrong'st it more than tears with that report.

35: **spake:** spoke

35: **to my face:** 1) she directed her insult to her own face and 2) she spoke it publicly

36: **mine:** refers to the idealized Renaissance concept that suggests marriage is the unification of two people into one; possibly also a reminder that Paris will control and have power over her

37: **it is not mine own:** Juliet appears to submit to Paris, but she means that it really is Romeo's, since he is her true husband.

40: **pensive:** sorrowfully thoughtful

Line 40: "My leisure serves me, pensive daughter, now": Henry Kolker as Friar Laurence, Norma Shearer as Juliet, and Ralph Forbes as Paris in George Cukor's 1936 movie production
Courtesy: Douglas Lanier

42: **shield:** forbid

48: **the compass of my wits:** my mental capabilities and resourcefulness

49: **prorogue:** delay

JULIET
  That is no slander, sir, which is a truth,
  And what I spake, I spake it to my face.   35

PARIS
  Thy face is mine, and thou hast slandered it.

JULIET
  It may be so, for it is not mine own.
  Are you at leisure, holy father, now,
  Or shall I come to you at evening mass?

FRIAR LAURENCE
  My leisure serves me, pensive daughter, now. —   40
  My lord, we must entreat the time alone.

PARIS
  God shield, I should disturb devotion. —
  Juliet, on Thursday early will I rouse ye.
  Till then, adieu, and keep this holy kiss.

                                        [*Exit PARIS*]

JULIET
  O shut the door, and when thou hast done so,   45
  Come weep with me, past hope, past cure, past help!

FRIAR LAURENCE
  O, Juliet, I already know thy grief.
  It strains me past the compass of my wits.
  I hear thou must, and nothing may prorogue it,
  On Thursday next be married to this County.   50

JULIET
  Tell me not, friar, that thou hearest of this,
  Unless thou tell me how I may prevent it.
  If, in thy wisdom, thou canst give no help,
  Do thou but call my resolution wise,
  And with this knife I'll help it presently.   55
  God joined my heart and Romeo's, thou our hands,

58: **label:** a seal appended to a deed

60: **both:** her hand and heart

61: **thy long-experienced time:** wisdom of your years

63: **extremes:** 1) extreme difficulties 2) extremities (i.e., parts of her body)

Lines 63–64: "'Twixt my extremes and me, this bloody knife / Shall play the umpire": Henry Kolker as Friar Laurence and Norma Shearer as Juliet in George Cukor's 1936 movie production
Courtesy: Douglas Lanier

65: **commission:** authority

75: **chide:** cast off

76: **cop'st:** meets

80: **thievish ways:** roads frequented by robbers

82: **charnel-house:** place where the bones of the dead are deposited

84: **reeky:** squalid and stinking

84: **shanks:** lower part of the leg, the calf

84: **chapless:** jawless

And ere this hand by thee to Romeo sealed,
Shall be the label to another deed,
Or my true heart with treacherous revolt
Turn to another, this shall sláy them both.   60
Therefore, out of thy long-experienced time,
Give me some present counsel, or, behold
'Twixt my extremes and me, this bloody knife
Shall play the umpire, arbitrating that
Which the commission of thy years and art   65
Could to no issue of true honour bring.
Be not so long to speak. I long to die
If what thou speak'st speak not of remedy.

FRIAR LAURENCE
Hold, daughter. I do spy a kind of hope
Which craves as desperate an execution   70
As that is desperate which we would prevent.
If, rather than to marry County Paris,
Thou hast the strength of will to slay thyself,
Then is it likely thou wilt undertake
. A thing like death to chide away this shame   75
That cop'st with death himself to scape from it.
And, if thou darest, I'll give thee remedy.

JULIET
O, bid me leap rather than marry Paris
From off the battlements of yonder tower,
Or walk in thievish ways, or bid me lurk   80
Where serpents are. Chain me with roaring bears,
Or shut me nightly in a charnel-house,
O'ercovered quite with dead men's rattling bones
With reeky shanks and yellow chapless skulls.
Or bid me go into a new-made grave   85
And hide me with a dead man in his shroud.
Things that, to hear them told, have made me tremble,
And I will do it without fear or doubt,
To live an unstained wife to my sweet love.

96: **when:** Then

97: **humour:** moisture, lethargy

98: **native progress:** natural heart rate

98: **surcease:** end

103: **supple government:** facility to maintain flexibility and control

105: **shrunk:** shrunken, shriveled

111: **bier:** funeral stand or open coffin used to transport the corpse to the tomb

114: **against:** before

115: **drift:** intention

120: **toy:** idle fancy

FRIAR LAURENCE
 Hold, then. Go home, be merry, give consent   90
 To marry Paris. Wednesday is tomorrow;
 Tomorrow night look that thou lie alone.
 Let not thy nurse lie with thee in thy chamber.
 Take thou this vial, being then in bed,
 And this distilled liquor drink thou off;   95
 When presently through all thy veins shall run
 A cold and drowsy humour, for no pulse
 Shall keep his native progress but surcease.
 No warmth, no breath, shall testify thou livest.
 The roses in thy lips and cheeks shall fade   100
 To many ashes, thy eyes' windows fall,
 Like death, when he shuts up the day of life.
 Each part, deprived of supple government,
 Shall, stiff and stark and cold, appear like death,
 And in this borrowed likeness of shrunk death,   105
 Thou shalt continue two and forty hours
 And then awake as from a pleasant sleep.
 Now, when the bridegroom in the morning comes
 To rouse thee from thy bed, there art thou dead.
 Then, as the manner of our country is,   110
 In thy best robes uncovered on the bier
 Thou shalt be borne to that same ancient vault
 Where all the kindred of the Capulets lie.
 In the meantime, against thou shalt awake,
 Shall Romeo by my letters know our drift,   115
 And hither shall he come, and he and I
 Will watch thy waking, and that very night
 Shall Romeo bear thee hence to Mantua.
 And this shall free thee from this present shame,
 If no inconstant toy nor womanish fear   120
 Abate thy valour in the acting it.

JULIET
 Give me, give me! O, tell not me of fear!

FRIAR LAURENCE
 Hold. Get you gone, be strong and prosperous

Julia Coffey as Juliet and Mike Nussbaum as Friar Laurence in Chicago Shakespeare
Theater's 2005 production, directed by Mark Lamos

Photo: Liz Lauren

In this resolve. I'll send a friar with speed
To Mantua with my letters to thy lord.   125

JULIET
Love give me strength, and strength shall help afford.
Farewell, dear father!

[Exeunt]

2: **cunning:** skillful

3: **try:** test

5: **'tis an ill cook...own fingers:** proverb

8: **unfurnished:** lacking necessities

10: **forsooth:** certainly

12: **harlotry:** wench

Act 4: Scene 2

*[Enter CAPULET, LADY CAPULET, NURSE,
and Servingmen, two or three]*

CAPULET
So many guests invite as here are writ.

[Exit First Servant]

Sirrah, go hire me twenty cunning cooks.

Second Servant
You shall have none ill, sir, for I'll try if they can lick their fingers.

CAPULET
How canst thou try them so?

Second Servant
Marry, sir, 'tis an ill cook that cannot lick his own fingers; therefore,   5
he that cannot lick his fingers goes not with me.

CAPULET
Go, be gone.

[Exit Second Servant]

We shall be much unfurnished for this time. —
What, is my daughter gone to Friar Laurence?

NURSE
Ay, forsooth.   10

CAPULET
Well, he may chance to do some good on her.
A peevish self-willed harlotry it is.

NURSE
See where she comes from shrift with merry look.

[Enter JULIET]

14: **headstrong:** i.e., headstrong girl

14: **gadding:** roaming, rambling idly

17: **enjoined:** ordered

24: **becomèd:** fitting and proper, appropriate

26: **on't:** of it

31: **closet:** private room or chamber

32: **needful:** necessary

33: **fit to furnish me:** proper for me to wear

CAPULET
  How now, my headstrong. Where have you been gadding?

JULIET
  Where I have learned me to repent the sin   15
  Of disobedient opposition
  To you and your behests and am enjoined
  By holy Laurence to fall prostrate here
  And beg your pardon. Pardon, I beseech you!
  Henceforward I am ever ruled by you.   20

CAPULET
  Send for the county; go tell him of this.
  I'll have this knot knit up tomorrow morning.

JULIET
  I met the youthful lord at Laurence' cell
  And gave him what becomèd love I might,
  Not stepping o'er the bounds of modesty.   25

CAPULET
  Why, I am glad on't. This is well. Stand up;
  This is as't should be. — Let me see the county;
  Ay, marry, go, I say, and fetch him hither. —
  Now, afore God, this reverend holy friar,
  Our whole city is much bound to him.   30

JULIET
  Nurse, will you go with me into my closet
  To help me sort such needful ornaments
  As you think fit to furnish me tomorrow?

LADY CAPULET
  No, not till Thursday. There is time enough.

CAPULET
  Go, Nurse, go with her. We'll to church tomorrow.   35
                              [*Exeunt JULIET and NURSE*]

38: **stir about:** busy myself

40: **deck up:** adorn, dress in finery

43: **forth:** off, away

45: **against:** in expectation of

LADY CAPULET
  We shall be short in our provision;
  'tis now near night.

CAPULET
                    Tush, I will stir about,
  And all things shall be well, I warrant thee, wife.
  Go thou to Juliet, help to deck up her.   40
  I'll not to bed tonight. Let me alone;
  I'll play the housewife for this once. — What, ho! —
  They are all forth. Well, I will walk myself
  To County Paris, to prepare up him
  Against tomorrow. My heart is wondrous light   45
  Since this same wayward girl is so reclaimed.

                                        [*Exeunt*]

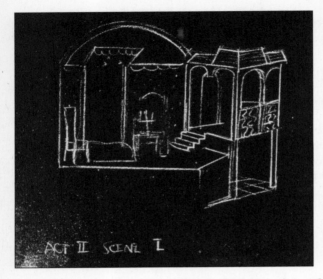

ACT II SCENE I

Scene: Juliet's Chamber: Set rendering of Juliet's bedroom from the New Theatre's 1935 production directed by Sir John Gielgud

3: **orisons:** prayers

4: **state:** condition

5: **cross:** abnormal, perverse

7: **culled:** picked out

7: **necessaries:** necessities

8: **behoveful:** fitting

Act 4: Scene 3]

[*Enter JULIET and NURSE*]

JULIET
  Ay, those attires are best, but, gentle nurse,
  I pray thee, leave me to myself tonight,
  For I have need of many orisons
  To move the heavens to smile upon my state,
  Which, well thou know'st, is cross and full of sin.   5
            [*Enter LADY CAPULET*]

LADY CAPULET
  What, are you busy, ho? Need you my help?

JULIET
  No, madam. We have culled such necessaries
  As are behoveful for our state tomorrow.
  So please you, let me now be left alone,
  And let the nurse this night sit up with you,   10
  For I am sure you have your hands full all
  In this so sudden business.

LADY CAPULET
          Good night.
  Get thee to bed, and rest, for thou hast need.
       [*Exeunt LADY CAPULET and NURSE*]

JULIET
  Farewell! God knows when we shall meet again.   15
  I have a faint cold fear thrills through my veins
  That almost freezes up the heat of life.
  I'll call them back again to comfort me.
  Nurse! What should she do here?
  My dismal scene I needs must act alone.   20
  Come, vial.   [*Takes out the vial*]
  What if this mixture do not work at all?

15–59:
Dame Peggy Ashcroft as Juliet
Virginia McKenna as Juliet
Ellen Terry as Juliet

26: **subtly:** deceitfully

30: **tried:** shown by experience to be

34: **stifled:** suffocated

37: **like:** likely

38: **conceit:** preconceived notions (nightmarish ones in this case)

43: **green in earth:** freshly buried

48: **mandrakes:** the plant Atropa mandragora which was thought to resemble the human figure and which was said to scream when torn from the ground, causing madness and even death

51: **environed with:** surrounded by

52: **joints:** bones

54: **rage:** raving madness

55: **dash out:** strike violently

57: **spit:** skewer (with a sword) as on a spit

Shall I be married then tomorrow morning?
No, no, this shall forbid it. Lie thou there.

[Laying down her dagger]

What if it be a poison, which the friar   25
Subtly hath ministered to have me dead,
Lest in this marriage he should be dishonoured
Because he married me before to Romeo?
I fear it is, and yet, methinks, it should not,
For he hath still been tried a holy man.   30
How if, when I am laid into the tomb,
I wake before the time that Romeo
Come to redeem me? There's a fearful point.
Shall I not, then, be stifled in the vault
To whose foul mouth no healthsome air breathes in,   35
And there die strangled ere my Romeo comes?
Or, if I live, is it not very like
The horrible conceit of death and night,
Together with the terror of the place,
As in a vault, an ancient receptacle,   40
Where, for these many hundred years, the bones
Of all my buried ancestors are packed;
Where bloody Tybalt, yet but green in earth,
Lies festering in his shroud; where, as they say,
At some hours in the night spirits, resort. —   45
Alack, alack, is it not like that I,
So early waking, what with loathsome smells
And shrieks like mandrakes torn out of the earth
That living mortals, hearing them, run mad. —
O, if I wake, shall I not be distraught,   50
Environed with all these hideous fears,
And madly play with my forefather's joints,
And pluck the mangled Tybalt from his shroud,
And, in this rage, with some great kinsman's bone,
As with a club, dash out my desperate brains?   55
O, look! Methinks I see my cousin's ghost
Seeking out Romeo that did spit his body
Upon a rapier's point. Stay, Tybalt, stay!
Romeo, I come! This do I drink to thee.

[She drinks and falls upon her bed, within the curtains]

2: **quinces:** pearlike fruits

7: **cot-quean:** a man who meddles in women's affairs and chores

9: **watching:** wakefulness

10: **not a whit:** not in the least

12: **mouse-hunt:** woman-chaser

14: **hood:** female/woman

Act 4: Scene 4]

[Enter LADY CAPULET and NURSE]

LADY CAPULET
Hold, take these keys and fetch more spices, nurse.

NURSE
They call for dates and quinces in the pastry.

[Enter old CAPULET]

CAPULET
Come, stir, stir, stir! The second cock hath crowed,
The curfew bell hath rung; 'tis three o'clock. —
Look to the baked meats, good Angelica.   5
Spare not for the cost.

NURSE
     Go, you cot-quean, go.
Get you to bed. Faith, you'll be sick to-morrow
For this night's watching.

CAPULET
No, not a whit. What, I have watched ere now   10
All night for lesser cause and ne'er been sick.

LADY CAPULET
Ay, you have been a mouse-hunt in your time,
But I will watch you from such watching now.
    [Exeunt LADY CAPULET and NURSE]

CAPULET
A jealous hood, a jealous hood!
  [Enter three or four Servingmen, with spits, logs, and baskets]
    Now, fellow,   15
What is there?

21: **find out logs:** i.e., know where to find logs (Capulet will pun on "logs" to suggest he is an idiot–see line 24)

23: **whoreson:** term of coarse familiarity ("bastard")

24: **loggerhead:** blockhead, dolt

25: **straight:** straightaway, momentarily

First Servant
    Things for the cook, sir, but I know not what.

CAPULET
    Make haste, make haste.

                                                  [Exit First Servant]
    Sirrah, fetch drier logs.
    Call Peter, he will show thee where they are.   20

Second Servant
    I have a head, sir, that will find out logs,
    And never trouble Peter for the matter.

                                                           [Exit]

CAPULET
    Mass, and well said. A merry whoreson, ha!
    Thou shalt be loggerhead. Good faith, 'tis day.

                                                 [Play music]
    The County will be here with music straight,   25
    For so he said he would. I hear him near. —
    Nurse! Wife! What, ho! What, nurse, I say!

                                            [Enter NURSE]
    Go waken Juliet; go and trim her up.
    I'll go and chat with Paris. Hie, make haste,
    Make haste! The bridegroom, he is come already.   30
    Make haste, I say.

                                                [Exeunt]

1: **fast:** i.e., fast asleep

2: **slug-a-bed:** lazy person

4: **pennyworths:** trifle, small amount (of sleep)

6: **set up his rest:** 1) phrase taken from gaming, meaning "have his weapon ready" (with a bawdy double entendre), and 2) is firmly resolved

10: **take you:** 1) surprise you 2) have sexual intercourse with you

15: **weraday:** exclamation of grief

16: **aqua vitae:** strong drink, spirits

Act 4: Scene 5

[*Enter NURSE*]

NURSE
Mistress! What, mistress! Juliet! — Fast, I warrant her, she. —
Why, lamb! Why, lady! Fie, you slug-a-bed!
Why, love, I say! Madam! Sweetheart! Why, bride!
What, not a word? You take your pennyworths now.
Sleep for a week, for the next night, I warrant,   5
The County Paris hath set up his rest
That you shall rest but little. — God forgive me.
Marry, and amen, how sound is she asleep!
I must needs wake her. — Madam, madam, madam!
Ay, let the county take you in your bed.   10
He'll fright you up, i' faith. Will it not be?
                                            [*Undraws the curtains*]
What, dressed, and in your clothes, and down again?
I must needs wake you. Lady, lady, lady! —
Alas, alas! Help, help! My lady's dead! —
O, weraday, that ever I was born! —   15
Some aqua vitae, ho! — My lord! My lady!
                                            [*Enter LADY CAPULET*]

LADY CAPULET
What noise is here?

NURSE
                        O lamentable day!

LADY CAPULET
What is the matter?

NURSE
                        Look, look! O heavy day!   20

27: **out:** used emphatically before *alack* and *alas*

38: **son:** i.e., Paris

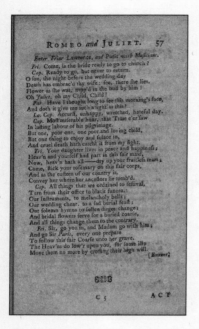

This is the whole of the rest of the scene in Garrick's production. The mourning for Juliet is continued in a new scene he created and inserted after this one: her funeral.

LADY CAPULET
  O me, O me! My child, my only life!
  Revive, look up, or I will die with thee!
  Help, help! Call help.

                                        [*Enter CAPULET*]

CAPULET
  For shame, bring Juliet forth; her lord is come.

NURSE
  She's dead, deceased, she's dead! Alack the day!   25

LADY CAPULET
  Alack the day! She's dead, she's dead, she's dead!

CAPULET
  Ha! let me see her. Out, alas, she's cold.
  Her blood is settled, and her joints are stiff.
  Life and these lips have long been separated.
  Death lies on her like an untimely frost   30
  Upon the sweetest flower of all the field.

NURSE
  O lamentable day!

LADY CAPULET
              O woeful time!

CAPULET
  Death that hath ta'en her hence to make me wail
  Ties up my tongue and will not let me speak.   35
  [*Enter FRIAR LAURENCE and the COUNTY PARIS, with Musicians*]

FRIAR LAURENCE
  Come, is the bride ready to go to church?

CAPULET
  Ready to go, but never to return.
  O son, the night before thy wedding-day

41: **deflowered:** 1) took her life and 2) took her virginity (as a husband would have)

47: **accursed:** cursed, doomed to misery

52: **catched:** taken, snatched

59: **spited:** maliciously thwarted

64: **uncomfortable:** joyless

Hath death lain with thy wife. There she lies,   40
Flower as she was, deflowered by him.
Death is my son-in-law; death is my heir.
My daughter he hath wedded. I will die
And leave him all. Life, living, all is Death's.

PARIS

Have I thought long to see this morning's face,   45
And doth it give me such a sight as this?

LADY CAPULET

Accursed, unhappy, wretched, hateful day!
Most miserable hour that e'er time saw
In lasting labour of his pilgrimage!
But one, poor one, one poor and loving child,   50
But one thing to rejoice and solace in,
And cruel death hath catched it from my sight!

NURSE

O woe! O woeful, woeful, woeful day!
Most lamentable day, most woeful day,
That ever, ever, I did yet behold!   55
O day! O day! O day! O hateful day!
Never was seen so black a day as this.
O woful day, O woful day!

PARIS

Beguiled, divorcèd, wrongèd, spited, slain!
Most detestable death, by thee beguiled,   60
By cruel, cruel thee quite overthrown!
O love! O life! Not life, but love in death!

CAPULET

Despised, distressèd, hated, martyred, killed!
Uncomfortable time, why camest thou now
To murder, murder our solemnity?   65
O child, O child, my soul and not my child!
Dead art thou. Alack, my child is dead,
And with my child my joys are burièd.

69: **confusion:** disaster, catastrophe

70: **confusions:** chaos, emotional upheavals

73: **your part in her:** i.e., her body

74: **his part:** i.e., her soul

75: **promotion:** i.e., social advancement

80: **well:** (when referring to the dead) at rest, free from the cares of the world

83: **rosemary:** herb which is a symbol of remembrance

84: **corse:** corpse, dead body

86: **fond:** foolish

87: **Yet nature...merriment:** logic laughs at nature's misfortunes

88: **festival:** be celebrated with joy

98: **lour:** frown

99: **move:** incite

FRIAR LAURENCE
   Peace, ho, for shame! Confusion's cure lives not
   In these confusions. Heaven and yourself   70
   Had part in this fair maid. Now, heaven hath all,
   And all the better is it for the maid.
   Your part in her you could not keep from death,
   But heaven keeps his part in eternal life.
   The most you sought was her promotion,   75
   For 'twas your heaven she should be advanced.
   And weep ye now, seeing she is advanced
   Above the clouds, as high as heaven itself?
   O, in this love, you love your child so ill
   That you run mad, seeing that she is well.   80
   She's not well married that lives married long,
   But she's best married that dies married young.
   Dry up your tears, and stick your rosemary
   On this fair corse, and, as the custom is,
   In all her best array bear her to church.   85
   For though fond nature bids us all lament,
   Yet nature's tears are reason's merriment.

CAPULET
   All things that we ordained festival
   Turn from their office to black funeral:
   Our instruments to melancholy bells,   90
   Our wedding cheer to a sad burial feast,
   Our solemn hymns to sullen dirges change,
   Our bridal flowers serve for a buried corse,
   And all things change them to the contrary.

FRIAR LAURENCE
   Sir, go you in, and, madam, go with him,   95
   And go, Sir Paris. Every one prepare
   To follow this fair corse unto her grave.
   The heavens do lour upon you for some ill;
   Move them no more by crossing their high will.
   [*Exeunt CAPULET, LADY CAPULET, PARIS, and FRIAR LAURENCE*]

First Musician
   Faith, we may put up our pipes and be gone.   100

102: **case:** situation

103: **case:** i.e., instrument case

104: **amended:** repaired

108: **dump:** melancholy song

112: **soundly:** 1) thoroughly (as a beating), and 2) pun on sound (as in a song)

114: **gleek:** a jeer or scoff

114: **minstrel:** one who sings or makes music for money (used as a slur)

115: **serving-creature:** servant (used in contempt)

NURSE
Honest good fellows, ah, put up, put up,
For, well you know, this is a pitiful case.

First Musician
Ay, by my troth, the case may be amended.

[*Exit NURSE*]
[*Enter PETER*]

PETER
Musicians, O musicians, "Heart's ease, Heart's ease." O, an you will
have me live, play "Heart's ease."   105

First Musician
Why "Heart's ease?"

PETER
O, musicians, because my heart itself plays "My heart is full." O, play me
some merry dump to comfort me.

First Musician
Not a dump, we. 'Tis no time to play now.

PETER
You will not, then?   110

First Musician
No.

PETER
I will then give it you soundly.

First Musician
What will you give us?

PETER
No money, on my faith, but the gleek; I will give you the minstrel.

First Musician
Then I will give you the serving-creature.   115

116: **pate:** the head (used in contempt)

116–117: **carry no crotchets:** i.e., not put up with your whims

117: **note:** understand, with a punning reference to a musical note

119: **put up:** put away

119: **put out:** pull out

120: **dry-beat:** thrash

122: **griping:** painful

123: **doleful dumps:** sorrowful songs (with a pun on dumps, meaning general sadness and melancholy)

126: **catling:** fiddle strings made of cat-gut (a derogatory nickname)

128: **rebeck:** a three-stringed fiddle

129: **sound for silver:** make music for money

130: **soundpost:** a small stick inserted between the top and the back of a violin (or fiddle) near the bridge

133: **gold:** payment, recompense

133: **sounding:** making music

135: **redress:** succor, help

PETER

Then will I lay the serving-creature's dagger on your pate. I will carry
no crotchets. I'll re you, I'll fa you; do you note me?

First Musician

An you re us and fa us, you note us.

Second Musician

Pray you, put up your dagger, and put out your wit.

PETER

Then have at you with my wit! I will dry-beat you with an iron   120
wit, and put up my iron dagger. Answer me like men:
    When griping grief the heart doth wound,
    And doleful dumps the mind oppress,
    Then music with her silver sound –
Why "silver sound?" Why "music with her silver sound?" What   125
say you, Simon Catling?

Musician

Marry, sir, because silver hath a sweet sound.

PETER

Prates! What say you, Hugh Rebeck?

Second Musician

I say "silver sound" because musicians sound for silver.

PETER

Prates too! What say you, James Soundpost?   130

Third Musician

Faith, I know not what to say.

PETER

O, I cry you mercy; you are the singer. I will say for you, it is "music with
her silver sound," because musicians have no gold for sounding.
    Then music with her silver sound
    With speedy help doth lend redress.   135
        [*Exit PETER*]

136: **pestilent knave:** disagreeable rascal

138: **stay:** stay for

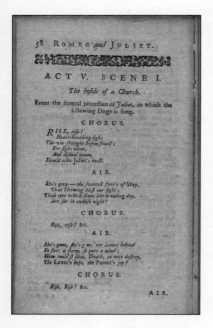

A new scene by Garrick: Juliet's funeral

First Musician

    What a pestilent knave is this same!

Second Musician

    Hang him, Jack. Come, we'll in here; tarry for the mourners and
stay dinner.

[Exeunt]

[Romeo and Juliet

Act 5

1: **flattering** : encouraging

Line 2: "My dreams presage some joyful news at hand": Patch Darragh as Romeo in the Guthrie Theater's 2004 production, directed by Ethan McSweeny
Photo: Michal Daniel

3: **my bosom's lord:** i.e., my heart

7: **leave:** permission

11: **shadows:** imagined pictures, dreams

18: **Capel's monument:** the Capulet family vault (burial place)

19: **immortal part:** i.e., soul

21: **took post:** used a post-horse, a horse stationed for the rapid conveyance of persons

Act 5: Scene 1]

[*Enter ROMEO*]

ROMEO
 If I may trust the flattering truth of sleep,
 My dreams presage some joyful news at hand.
 My bosom's lord sits lightly in his throne,
 And all this day an unaccustomed spirit
 Lifts me above the ground with cheerful thoughts.   5
 I dreamt my lady came and found me dead —
 Strange dream, that gives a dead man leave to think —
 And breathed such life with kisses in my lips
 That I revived and was an emperor.
 Ah me, how sweet is love itself possessed,   10
 When but love's shadows are so rich in joy!
               [*Enter Romeo's man, BALTHASAR, booted*]
 News from Verona! — How now, Balthasar!
 Dost thou not bring me letters from the friar?
 How doth my lady? Is my father well?
 How fares my Juliet? That I ask again,   15
 For nothing can be ill, if she be well.

BALTHASAR
 Then she is well, and nothing can be ill.
 Her body sleeps in Capel's monument,
 And her immortal part with angels lives.
 I saw her laid low in her kindred's vault,   20
 And presently took post to tell it you.
 O, pardon me for bringing these ill news,
 Since you did leave it for my office, sir.

ROMEO
 Is it e'en so? Then I defy you, stars!
 Thou know'st my lodging; get me ink and paper,   25
 And hire post-horses. I will hence tonight.

37: **for means:** about a method

39: **apothecary:** a druggist/chemist, one who deals in medicine and herbal remedies

41: **tattered weeds:** torn, ragged garments

41: **overwhelming:** overhanging, as in one who frowns

42: **culling of simples:** selecting (culling) medicinal herbs (simples)

44: **needy:** very poor

44–46: **tortoise/alligator/fishes:** traditional ornaments in an apothecary's shop

47: **beggarly account:** poor display

49: **packthread:** thread used in tying up parcels

49: **cakes of roses:** preparation of rose-petals in the form of a cake, used as a perfume

53: **Whose sale is present death:** The sale (of poison) is punishable by immediate death

54: **caitiff:** miserable

55: **forerun:** precede

BALTHASAR
  I do beseech you, sir, have patience.
  Your looks are pale and wild and do import
  Some misadventure.

ROMEO
                Tush, thou art deceived.   30
  Leave me, and do the thing I bid thee do.
  Hast thou no letters to me from the friar?

BALTHASAR
  No, my good lord.

ROMEO
             No matter. Get thee gone,
  And hire those horses. I'll be with thee straight.   35
                            [Exit BALTHASAR]

  Well, Juliet, I will lie with thee tonight.
  Let's see for means. O mischief, thou art swift
  To enter in the thoughts of desperate men.
  I do remember an apothecary, —
  And hereabouts he dwells, — which late I noted   40
  In tattered weeds, with overwhelming brows,
  Culling of simples. Meager were his looks;
  Sharp misery had worn him to the bones.
  And in his needy shop a tortoise hung,
  An alligator stuffed, and other skins   45
  Of ill-shaped fishes; and about his shelves,
  A beggarly account of empty boxes,
  Green earthen pots, bladders and musty seeds,
  Remnants of packthread, and old cakes of roses
  Were thinly scattered to make up a show.   50
  Noting this penury, to myself I said,
  "An if a man did need a poison now,
  Whose sale is present death in Mantua,
  Here lives a caitiff wretch would sell it him."
  O, this same thought did but forerun my need,   55
  And this same needy man must sell it me.
  As I remember, this should be the house.

62: **ducats:** gold coins

63: **dram:** a small amount, one-eighth of a fluid ounce

63: **soon-speeding gear:** quickly effective poison

66: **trunk:** the body of an animal, especially of man

70: **utters:** causes to pass from one hand to another

76: **affords:** grants, offers

Being holiday, the beggar's shop is shut.
What, ho! Apothecary!

[Enter APOTHECARY]

APOTHECARY
                    Who calls so loud?   60

ROMEO
Come hither, man. I see that thou art poor.
Hold, there is forty ducats. Let me have
A dram of poison, such soon-speeding gear
As will disperse itself through all the veins
That the life-weary taker may fall dead   65
And that the trunk may be discharged of breath
As violently as hasty powder fired
Doth hurry from the fatal cannon's womb.

APOTHECARY
Such mortal drugs I have; but Mantua's law
Is death to any he that utters them.   70

ROMEO
Art thou so bare and full of wretchedness
And fear'st to die? Famine is in thy cheeks;
Need and oppression starveth in thine eyes;
Contempt and beggary hangs upon thy back.
The world is not thy friend nor the world's law. 75
The world affords no law to make thee rich.
Then be not poor, but break it and take this.

APOTHECARY
My poverty, but not my will, consents.

ROMEO
I pay thy poverty and not thy will.

APOTHECARY
Put this in any liquid thing you will,   80
And drink it off, and, if you had the strength
Of twenty men, it would dispatch you straight.

83–84: worse poison...loathsome world: i.e., gold causes more murders than this illegal poison does, and therefore gold is more dangerous.

Line 83: "There is thy gold, worse poison to men's souls": Ian Wolfe as Apothecary and Leslie Howard as Romeo in George Cukor's 1936 movie production
Courtesy: Douglas Lanier

87: get thyself in flesh: fatten yourself up

88: cordial: a medicine raising the spirits

ROMEO
    There is thy gold, worse poison to men's souls,
    Doing more murders in this loathsome world,
    Than these poor compounds that thou mayst not sell.   85
    I sell thee poison; thou hast sold me none.
    Farewell. Buy food, and get thyself in flesh.
    Come, cordial and not poison, go with me
    To Juliet's grave, for there must I use thee.

                                     [Exeunt]

5: **barefoot brother:** i.e., another friar

6: **associate me:** accompany me

8: **searchers:** paid officials who sought out and identified plague victims

10: **pestilence:** plague

12: **stayed:** stopped

18: **nice:** light, unimportant

18: **charge:** weight, importance

19: **dear import:** great importance

Act 5: Scene 2

[Enter FRIAR JOHN]

FRIAR JOHN
Holy Franciscan friar! Brother, ho!

[Enter FRIAR LAURENCE]

FRIAR LAURENCE
This same should be the voice of Friar John.
Welcome from Mantua; what says Romeo?
Or, if his mind be writ, give me his letter.

FRIAR JOHN
Going to find a barefoot brother out,   5
One of our order to associate me,
Here in this city visiting the sick,
And finding him, the searchers of the town,
Suspecting that we both were in a house
Where the infectious pestilence did reign,   10
Sealed up the doors and would not let us forth,
So that my speed to Mantua there was stayed.

FRIAR LAURENCE
Who bare my letter, then, to Romeo?

FRIAR JOHN
I could not send it, — here it is again, —
Nor get a messenger to bring it thee,   15
So fearful were they of infection.

FRIAR LAURENCE
Unhappy fortune! By my brotherhood,
The letter was not nice but full of charge
Of dear import, and the neglecting it
May do much danger. Friar John, go hence.   20

21: **iron crow:** crowbar

26: **beshrew:** mildly curse

27: **accidents:** events

30: **corse:** body (i.e., Juliet)

Get me an iron crow, and bring it straight
Unto my cell.

FRIAR JOHN
                              Brother, I'll go and bring it thee.

[Exit]

FRIAR LAURENCE
    Now must I to the monument alone.
    Within three hours will fair Juliet wake.   25
    She will beshrew me much that Romeo
    Hath had no notice of these accidents,
    But I will write again to Mantua,
    And keep her at my cell till Romeo come.
    Poor living corse, closed in a dead man's tomb!   30

[Exit]

1: **aloof:** at a distance

3: **yew trees:** planted in churchyards, and therefore emblem of death

11: **adventure:** dare, hazard

Line 13: "O woe! Thy canopy is dust and stones": Lee Mark Nelson as Paris and
Christine Marie Brown as Juliet in the Guthrie Theater's 2004 production directed
by Ethan McSweeny
Photo: Michal Daniel

14: **sweet:** perfumed

16: **obsequies:** dutiful acts performed in memory of one who has died

20: **cross:** thwart, hinder

21: **muffle me:** hide me, cover me

Act 5: Scene 3

[*Enter PARIS and his Page, bearing flowers and a torch*]

PARIS
    Give me thy torch, boy. Hence, and stand aloof.
    Yet put it out, for I would not be seen.
    Under yond yew trees lay thee all along,
    Holding thy ear close to the hollow ground.
    So shall no foot upon the churchyard tread,   5
    Being loose, unfirm with digging up of graves,
    But thou shalt hear it. Whistle then to me,
    As signal that thou hear'st something approach.
    Give me those flowers. Do as I bid thee, go.

PAGE
    [*Aside*] I am almost afraid to stand alone   10
    Here in the churchyard. Yet I will adventure.

                [*Retires*]

PARIS
    Sweet flower, with flowers thy bridal bed I strew, —
    O woe! Thy canopy is dust and stones. —
    Which with sweet water nightly I will dew,
    Or, wanting that, with tears distilled by moans.   15
    The obsequies that I for thee will keep
    Nightly shall be to strew thy grave and weep.

                [*The Page whistles*]

    The boy gives warning something doth approach.
    What cursèd foot wanders this way tonight
    To cross my obsequies and true love's rite?   20
    What, with a torch? Muffle me, night, awhile.

                [*Retires*]
    [*Enter ROMEO and BALTHASAR*]

22: **mattock:** kind of pickaxe

32: **dear employment:** valuable or important business

33: **jealous:** suspicious in any way

37: **savage-wild:** cruel, ferocious

45: **detestable maw:** i.e., the grave (maw = throat or gaping mouth)

ROMEO

Give me that mattock and the wrenching iron.
Hold, take this letter. Early in the morning
See thou deliver it to my lord and father.
Give me the light. Upon thy life, I charge thee,   25
Whate'er thou hear'st or seest, stand all aloof,
And do not interrupt me in my course.
Why I descend into this bed of death
Is partly to behold my lady's face,
But chiefly to take thence from her dead finger   30
A precious ring, a ring that I must use
In dear employment. Therefore hence, be gone.
But if thou, jealous, dost return to pry
In what I further shall intend to do,
By heaven, I will tear thee joint by joint   35
And strew this hungry churchyard with thy limbs.
The time and my intents are savage-wild,
More fierce and more inexorable far
Than empty tigers or the roaring sea.

BALTHASAR

I will be gone, sir, and not trouble you.   40

ROMEO

So shalt thou show me friendship. Take thou that.
Live and be prosperous, and farewell, good fellow.

BALTHASAR

[*Aside*] For all this same, I'll hide me hereabout.
His looks I fear, and his intents I doubt.

                                                            [*Retires*]

ROMEO

Thou detestable maw, thou womb of death,   45
Gorged with the dearest morsel of the earth.
Thus I enforce thy rotten jaws to open,
And, in despite, I'll cram thee with more food.

                                              [*Opens the tomb*]

54: **unhallowed:** unholy, wicked

60: **these gone:** the dead (i.e., Juliet and Tybalt)

61: **affright:** terrify

65: **armed against myself:** i.e., with poison to kill myself

68: **conjurations:** solemn appeals or entreaties

73: **merciful:** compassionate

PARIS
> This is that banished haughty Montague
> That murdered my love's cousin, with which grief,   50
> It is supposed, the fair creature died,
> And here is come to do some villainous shame
> To the dead bodies. I will apprehend him.

[Comes forward]

> Stop thy unhallowed toil, vile Montague!
> Can vengeance be pursued further than death?   55
> Condemned villain, I do apprehend thee.
> Obey, and go with me, for thou must die.

ROMEO
> I must indeed, and therefore came I hither.
> Good gentle youth, tempt not a desperate man.
> Fly hence, and leave me. Think upon these gone;   60
> Let them affright thee. I beseech thee, youth,
> Put not another sin upon my head,
> By urging me to fury. O, be gone!
> By heaven, I love thee better than myself,
> For I come hither armed against myself.   65
> Stay not, begone. Live, and hereafter say
> A madman's mercy bade thee run away.

PARIS
> I do defy thy conjurations
> And apprehend thee for a felon here.

ROMEO
> Wilt thou provoke me? Then, have at thee, boy!   70

[They fight]

PAGE
> O Lord, they fight! I will go call the watch.

[Exit]

PARIS
> O, I am slain!

[Falls]

> If thou be merciful,
> Open the tomb, lay me with Juliet.

[Dies]

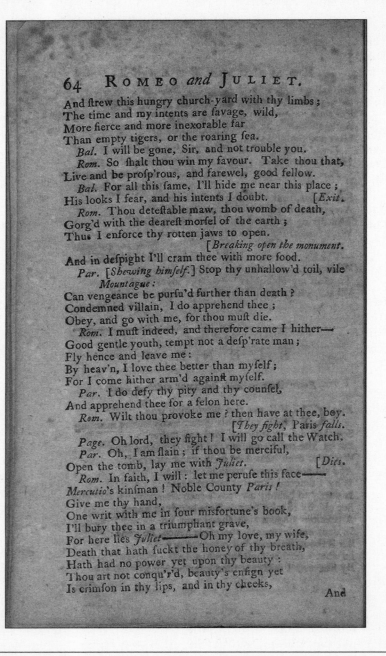

64   R O M E O *and* J U L I E T.

And ſtrew this hungry church-yard with thy limbs;
The time and my intents are ſavage, wild,
More fierce and more inexorable far
Than empty tigers, or the roaring ſea.

 Bal. I will be gone, Sir, and not trouble you.
 Rom. So ſhalt thou win my favour. Take thou that,
Live and be proſp'rous, and farewel, good fellow.
 Bal. For all this ſame, I'll hide me near this place;
His looks I fear, and his intents I doubt.   [*Exit.*
 Rom. Thou deteſtable maw, thou womb of death,
Gorg'd with the deareſt morſel of the earth;
Thus I enforce thy rotten jaws to open.
      [*Breaking open the monument.*
And in deſpight I'll cram thee with more food.
 Par. [*Shewing himſelf.*] Stop thy unhallow'd toil, vile
  Mountague:
Can vengeance be purſu'd further than death?
Condemned villain, I do apprehend thee;
Obey, and go with me, for thou muſt die.
 Rom. I muſt indeed, and therefore came I hither——
Good gentle youth, tempt not a deſp'rate man;
Fly hence and leave me:
By heav'n, I love thee better than myſelf;
For I come hither arm'd againſt myſelf.
 Par. I do defy thy pity and thy counſel,
And apprehend thee for a felon here.
 Rom. Wilt thou provoke me? then have at thee, boy.
      [*They fight*, Paris *falls.*
 Page. Oh lord, they fight! I will go call the Watch.
 Par. Oh, I am ſlain; if thou be merciful,
Open the tomb, lay me with *Juliet.*   [*Dies.*
 Rom. In faith, I will: let me peruſe this face——
Mercutio's kinſman! Noble County *Paris!*
Give me thy hand,
One writ with me in ſour misfortune's book,
I'll bury thee in a triumphant grave,
For here lies *Juliet*——Oh my love, my wife,
Death that hath ſuckt the honey of thy breath,
Hath had no power yet upon thy beauty:
Thou art not conqu'r'd, beauty's enſign yet
Is crimſon in thy lips, and in thy cheeks,
          And

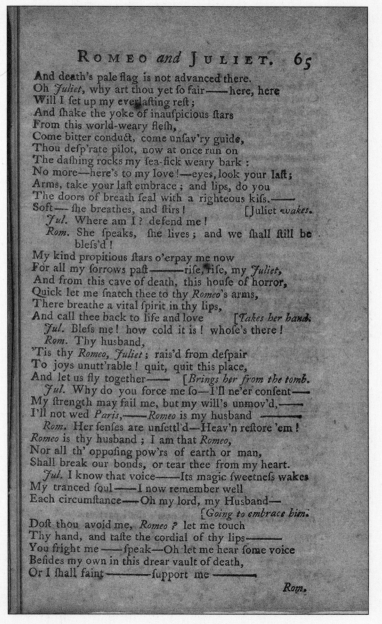

ROMEO *and* JULIET.   65

And death's pale flag is not advanced there.
Oh *Juliet*, why art thou yet so fair——here, here
Will I set up my everlasting rest;
And shake the yoke of inauspicious stars
From this world-weary flesh,
Come bitter conduct, come unsav'ry guide,
Thou desp'rate pilot, now at once run on
The dashing rocks my sea-sick weary bark:
No more——here's to my love!——eyes, look your last;
Arms, take your last embrace; and lips, do you
The doors of breath seal with a righteous kiss.——
Soft——she breathes, and stirs!   [*Juliet wakes.*
   Jul. Where am I? defend me!
   Rom. She speaks, she lives; and we shall still be .
      bless'd!
My kind propitious stars o'erpay me now
For all my sorrows past——rise, rise, my *Juliet*,
And from this cave of death, this house of horror,
Quick let me snatch thee to thy *Romeo*'s arms,
There breathe a vital spirit in thy lips,
And call thee back to life and love   [*Takes her hand.*
   Jul. Bless me! how cold it is! whose's there!
   Rom. Thy husband,
'Tis thy *Romeo*, *Juliet*; rais'd from despair
To joys unutt'rable! quit, quit this place,
And let us fly together——   [*Brings her from the tomb.*
   Jul. Why do you force me so——I'll ne'er consent——
My strength may fail me, but my will's unmov'd,——
I'll not wed *Paris*,——*Romeo* is my husband——
   Rom. Her senses are unsettl'd——Heav'n restore 'em!
Romeo is thy husband; I am that *Romeo*,
Nor all th' opposing pow'rs of earth or man,
Shall break our bonds, or tear thee from my heart.
   Jul. I know that voice——Its magic sweetness wakes
My tranced soul——I now remember well
Each circumstance——Oh my lord, my Husband—
                      [*Going to embrace him.*
Dost thou avoid me, *Romeo* ? let me touch
Thy hand, and taste the cordial of thy lips——
You fright me——speak—Oh let me hear some voice
Besides my own in this drear vault of death,
Or I shall faint——support me ——

                                        Rom.

David Garrick's inserted scene: Juliet wakes before Romeo dies
Furness Shakespeare Library

66   ROMEO *and* JULIET.

Rom. Oh I cannot,
I have no ſtrength, but want thy feeble aid,
Cruel poiſon!
  Jul. Poiſon! what means my lord ; thy trembling
      voice!
Pale lips!, and ſwimming eyes! death's in thy face!
  Rom. It is indeed———I ſtruggle with him now———
The tranſports that I felt, to hear thee ſpeak,
And ſee thy op'ning eyes, ſtopt for a moment
His inpetuous courſe, and all my mind
Was happineſs and thee; but now the poiſon
Ruſhes thro' my veins———I've not time to tell———
Fate brought me to this place———to take a laſt,
Laſt farewel of my love and with thee die.
  Jul. Die? was the *Friar* falſe!
  Rom. I know not that———
I thought thee dead; diſtracted at the ſight,
(Fatal ſpeed) drank poiſon, kiſs'd thy cold lips,
And found within thy arms a precious grave———
But in that momen———Oh
  Jul. And did I wake for this!
  Rom. My powers are blaſted,
'Twixt death and love I'm torn———I am diſtracted!
But death's ſtrongeſt—and muſt I leave thee, *Juliet!*
Oh cruel curſed fate! in ſight of heav'n———
  Jul. Thou rav'ſt———lean on my breaſt———
  Rom. Fathers have flinty hearts, no tears can melt
      'em.
Nature pleads in vain—Children muſt be wretched———
  Jul. Oh my breaking heart———
  Rom. She is my wife—our hearts are twin'd together——
Capulet, forbear———*Paris,* looſe your hold———
Pull not our heart-ſtrings thus———they crack———they
      break———
Oh *Juliet! Juliet!*   [*Dies.*
  Jul. Stay, ſtay, for me, *Romeo*———
A moment ſtay; fate marries us in death,
And we are *one*——— no pow'r ſhall part us.
                    [*Faints on* Romeo's *body.*

                                    Enter

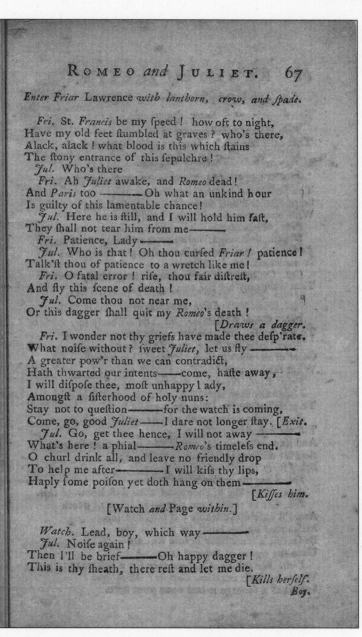

ROMEO *and* JULIET. 67

Enter Friar Lawrence *with lanthorn, crow, and spade.*

Fri. St. *Francis* be my speed! how oft to night,
Have my old feet stumbled at graves? who's there,
Alack, alack! what blood is this which stains
The stony entrance of this sepulchre!
  Jul. Who's there
  Fri. Ah *Juliet* awake, and *Romeo* dead!
And *Paris* too ———— Oh what an unkind hour
Is guilty of this lamentable chance!
  Jul. Here he is still, and I will hold him fast,
They shall not tear him from me————
  Fri. Patience, Lady————
  Jul. Who is that! Oh thou cursed *Friar!* patience!
Talk'st thou of patience to a wretch like me!
  Fri. O fatal error! rise, thou fair distrest,
And fly this scene of death!
  Jul. Come thou not near me,
Or this dagger shall quit my *Romeo*'s death!
                              [*Draws a dagger.*
  Fri. I wonder not thy griefs have made thee desp'rate.
What noise without? sweet *Juliet,* let us fly————
A greater pow'r than we can contradict,
Hath thwarted our intents——come, haste away,
I will dispose thee, most unhappy lady,
Amongst a sisterhood of holy nuns:
Stay not to question——for the watch is coming,
Come, go, good *Juliet*——I dare not longer stay. [*Exit.*
  Jul. Go, get thee hence, I will not away————
What's here! a phial——*Romeo*'s timeless end.
O churl drink all, and leave no friendly drop
To help me after——I will kiss thy lips,
Haply some poison yet doth hang on them————
                              [*Kisses him.*

[*Watch and* Page *within.*]

  Watch. Lead, boy, which way————
  Jul. Noise again!
Then I'll be brief——Oh happy dagger!
This is thy sheath, there rest and let me die.
                              [*Kills herself.*
                              Boy.

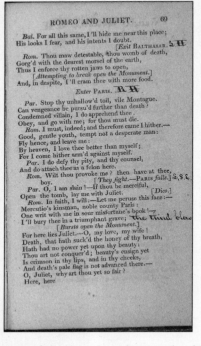

ROMEO AND JULIET. 69

Bal. For all this same, I'll hide me near this place;
His looks I fear, and his intents I doubt.
                     [*Exit* BALTHASAR.
Rom. Thou maw detestable, thou womb of death,
Gorg'd with the dearest morsel of the earth,
Thus I enforce thy rotten jaws to open,
      [*Attempting to break open the Monument.*]
And, in despite, I'll cram thee with more food.
            Enter PARIS.
Par. Stop thy unhallow'd toil, vile Montague.
Can vengeance be pursu'd further than death?
Condemned villain, I do apprehend thee.
Obey, and go with me; for thou must die.
Rom. I must, indeed; and therefore came I hither.—
Good, gentle youth, tempt not a desperate man:
Fly hence, and leave me:
By heaven, I love thee better than myself;
For I come hither arm'd against myself.
Par. I do defy thy pity, and thy counsel,
And do attach thee as a felon here.
Rom. Wilt thou provoke me? then have at thee,
   boy.   [*They fight.*—PARIS *falls.*]
Par. O, I am slain!—If thou be merciful,
Open the tomb, lay me with Juliet.   [*Dies.*]
Rom. In faith, I will:—Let me peruse this face:—
Mercutio's kinsman, noble county Paris:
One writ with me in sour misfortune's book!—
I'll bury thee in a triumphant grave;
          [*Bursts open the Monument.*]
For here lies Juliet.—O, my love, my wife!
Death, that hath suck'd the honey of thy breath,
Hath had no power yet upon thy beauty:
Thou art not conquer'd; beauty's ensign yet
Is crimson in thy lips, and in thy cheeks,
And death's pale flag is not advanced there.—
O, Juliet, why art thou yet so fair?
Here, here

Romeo's lines 77–82, indicating that his man told him Paris was to marry Juliet, do not appear in J. P. Kemble's text

77: **betossèd:** agitated
78: **attend:** notice
84: **triumphant:** of supreme magnificence and beauty
85: **lantern:** a glass-enclosed room
87: **feasting presence:** chamber or state room where feasts are held
88: **by a dead man interred:** buried by a dead man (i.e., by Romeo, who is as good as dead)
91: **lightning:** revelation
95: **ensign:** banner, sign
104: **unsubstantial:** immaterial, incorporeal

ROMEO

In faith, I will. Let me peruse this face.   75
Mercutio's kinsman, noble County Paris!
What said my man when my betossèd soul
Did not attend him as we rode? I think
He told me Paris should have married Juliet.
Said he not so, or did I dream it so?   80
Or am I mad, hearing him talk of Juliet,
To think it was so? O, give me thy hand,
One writ with me in sour misfortune's book!
I'll bury thee in a triumphant grave.
A grave? O no! A lantern, slaughtered youth,   85
For here lies Juliet, and her beauty makes
This vault a feasting presence full of light.
Death, lie thou there, by a dead man interred.

[Laying PARIS in the tomb]

How oft when men are at the point of death
Have they been merry, which their keepers call   90
A lightning before death. Oh how may I
Call this a lightning? O my love, my wife,
Death, that hath sucked the honey of thy breath,
Hath had no power yet upon thy beauty.
Thou art not conquered. Beauty's ensign yet   95
Is crimson in thy lips and in thy cheeks,
And death's pale flag is not advanced there.
Tybalt, liest thou there in thy bloody sheet?
O, what more favour can I do to thee,
Than with that hand that cut thy youth in twain   100
To sunder his that was thine enemy?
Forgive me, cousin! Ah, dear Juliet,
Why art thou yet so fair? Shall I believe
That unsubstantial death is amorous,
And that the lean abhorred monster keeps   105
Thee here in dark to be his paramour?
For fear of that, I still will stay with thee,
And never from this palace of dim night
Depart again. Here, here will I remain
With worms that are thy chambermaids. O, here   110
Will I set up my everlasting rest,

112: **inauspicious stars:** unfavorable fortune

116: **dateless:** eternal

116: **engrossing:** all-encompassing

117: **conduct:** guide or escort

118: **desperate pilot:** Romeo is referring to himself

119: **bark:** ship

123: **be my speed:** assist me on my way

And shake the yoke of inauspicious stars
From this world-wearied flesh. Eyes, look your last.
Arms, take your last embrace. And, lips, O you
The doors of breath, seal with a righteous kiss   115
A dateless bargain to engrossing death.
Come, bitter conduct, come, unsavoury guide!
Thou desperate pilot, now at once run on
The dashing rocks thy seasick weary bark!
Here's to my love!   120

[Drinks]

O true Apothecary!
Thy drugs are quick. Thus with a kiss I die.

[Dies]
[Enter FRIAR LAURENCE with a lantern, crow, and spade]

FRIAR LAURENCE
    Saint Francis be my speed! How oft tonight
    Have my old feet stumbled at graves. Who's there?

BALTHASAR
    Here's one, a friend, and one that knows you well.   125

FRIAR LAURENCE
    Bliss be upon you! Tell me, good my friend,
    What torch is yond that vainly lends his light
    To grubs and eyeless skulls? As I discern,
    It burneth in the Capel's monument.

BALTHASAR
    It doth so, holy sir, and there's my master,   130
    One that you love.

FRIAR LAURENCE
                    Who is it?

BALTHASAR
                    Romeo.

Line 151: "Romeo! O, pale! Who else?": Henry Kolker as Friar Laurence, Leslie Howard as Romeo, and Norma Shearer as Juliet in George Cukor's 1936 movie production
Courtesy: Douglas Lanier

153: **lamentable chance:** unhappy event

FRIAR LAURENCE
    How long hath he been there?

BALTHASAR
                Full half an hour.   135

FRIAR LAURENCE
    Go with me to the vault.

BALTHASAR
                I dare not, sir
    My master knows not but I am gone hence,
    And fearfully did menace me with death
    If I did stay to look on his intents.   140

FRIAR LAURENCE
    Stay, then. I'll go alone. Fear comes upon me.
    O, much I fear some ill unthrifty thing.

BALTHASAR
    As I did sleep under this yew tree here,
    I dreamt my master and another fought,
    And that my master slew him.   145

FRIAR LAURENCE
            Romeo!

                              [Advances]

    Alack, alack, what blood is this, which stains
    The stony entrance of this sepulchre?
    What mean these masterless and gory swords
    To lie discoloured by this place of peace?   150
                          [Enters the tomb]

    Romeo! O, pale! Who else? What, Paris too?
    And steeped in blood? Ah, what an unkind hour
    Is guilty of this lamentable chance?
    The lady stirs.

                            [JULIET wakes]

155: **comfortable:** inclined to help, benevolent

Lines 158–159: "I hear some noise. Lady, come from that nest / Of death": Joseph Marcell as Friar Lawrence and Jennifer Ikeda as Juliet in The Shakespeare Theatre's 2001-2002 production directed by Rachel Kavanaugh
Photo: Carol Rosegg

170: **timeless:** untimely, premature

171: **churl:** peasant, rude and ill-bred fellow

173: **haply:** perhaps

177: **happy:** propitious, fortuitous

JULIET

    O comfortable friar, where is my lord?   155
    I do remember well where I should be,
    And there I am. Where is my Romeo?

                                [Noise within]

FRIAR LAURENCE

    I hear some noise. Lady, come from that nest
    Of death, contagion, and unnatural sleep.
    A greater power than we can contradict   160
    Hath thwarted our intents. Come, come away.
    Thy husband in thy bosom there lies dead
    And Paris too. Come, I'll dispose of thee
    Among a sisterhood of holy nuns.
    Stay not to question, for the watch is coming.   165
    Come, go, good Juliet,

                                [Noise again]

    I dare no longer stay.

JULIET

    Go, get thee hence, for I will not away.

                   [Exit FRIAR LAURENCE]

    What's here? A cup, closed in my true love's hand?
    Poison, I see, hath been his timeless end.   170
    O churl, drunk all, and left no friendly drop
    To help me after? I will kiss thy lips.
    Haply some poison yet doth hang on them
    To make me die with a restorative.

                              [Kisses him]

    Thy lips are warm.   175

First Watchman

                              [Within]

          Lead, boy. Which way?

JULIET

    Yea, noise? Then I'll be brief. O happy dagger!

                [Snatching ROMEO's dagger]

    This is thy sheath.

Line 179: "There rust and let me die": Olivia Hussey as Juliet and Leonard Whiting
as Romeo in Franco Zeffirelli's 1968 movie production
Courtesy: Douglas Lanier

182: **attach:** seize

188: **ground:** reason, cause

190: **circumstance:** particulars, details

190: **descry:** discover

194: **mattock:** a kind of pick-axe

196: **stay:** detain

[Stabs herself]

There rust and let me die.

[Falls on ROMEO's body and dies]
[Enter Watch, with the Page of PARIS]

PAGE
This is the place, there where the torch doth burn.   180

First Watchman
The ground is bloody. Search about the churchyard.
Go, some of you, whoe'er you find, attach.
Pitiful sight! Here lies the county slain,
And Juliet bleeding, warm, and newly dead,
Who here hath lain these two days buried.   185
Go, tell the Prince. Run to the Capulets.
Raise up the Montagues. Some others search.
We see the ground whereon these woes do lie,
But the true ground of all these piteous woes
We cannot without circumstance descry.   190
[Enter some of the Watch with Romeo's man, BALTHASAR]

Second Watchman
Here's Romeo's man; we found him in the churchyard.

First Watchman
Hold him in safety till the prince come hither.
[Enter others of the Watch with FRIAR LAURENCE]

Third Watchman
Here is a friar, that trembles, sighs and weeps.
We took this mattock and this spade from him
As he was coming from this churchyard's side.   195

First Watchman
A great suspicion. Stay the friar too.
[Enter the PRINCE and Attendants]

PRINCE
What misadventure is so early up
That calls our person from our morning rest?

199: **shrieked abroad:** call out or shout in public

202: **monument:** tomb

212: **his house:** i.e., the dagger's sheath

218: **now early down:** i.e., dead earlier (than Montague's early wakening)

[Enter CAPULET and LADY CAPULET]

CAPULET
What should it be, that is so shrieked abroad?

LADY CAPULET
O the people in the street cry Romeo,   200
Some Juliet, and some Paris, and all run
With open outcry toward our monument.

PRINCE
What fear is this which startles in our ears?

First Watchman
Sovereign, here lies the County Paris slain,
And Romeo dead, and Juliet, dead before,   205
Warm and new killed.

PRINCE
Search, seek, and know how this foul murder comes.

First Watchman
Here is a friar and slaughtered Romeo's man
With instruments upon them, fit to open
These dead men's tombs.   210

CAPULET
O heavens! O wife, look how our daughter bleeds!
This dagger hath mista'en, for, lo, his house
Is empty on the back of Montague,
And it mis-sheathed in my daughter's bosom!

LADY CAPULET
O me! This sight of death is as a bell   215
That warns my old age to a sepulchre.

[Enter MONTAGUE]

PRINCE
Come, Montague, for thou art early up
To see thy son and heir now early down.

223: **untaught:** unmannerly

224: **to press...a grave:** i.e., to die before your father

225: **seal up the mouth of outrage:** i.e., silence yourself

228: **general of your woes:** leader of your lamentations

230: **mischance:** misfortune

232: **the greatest:** i.e., the most suspicious

232: **able to do least:** because he was not able to prevent the tragedy

234: **direful:** dismal

235: **purge:** clear from crime

242: **stol'n:** stolen i.e., secret, furtive

MONTAGUE
    Alas, my liege, my wife is dead tonight.
    Grief of my son's exile hath stopped her breath.   220
    What further woe conspires against mine age?

PRINCE
    Look, and thou shalt see.

MONTAGUE
    O thou untaught! What manners is in this
    To press before thy father to a grave?

PRINCE
    Seal up the mouth of outrage for a while,   225
    Till we can clear these ambiguities,
    And know their spring, their head, their true descent,
    And then will I be general of your woes,
    And lead you even to death. Meantime, forbear,
    And let mischance be slave to patience.   230
    Bring forth the parties of suspicion.

FRIAR LAURENCE
    I am the greatest, able to do least,
    Yet most suspected, as the time and place
    Doth make against me of this direful murder.
    And here I stand, both to impeach and purge   235
    Myself condemnèd and myself excused.

PRINCE
    Then say at once what thou dost know in this.

FRIAR LAURENCE
    I will be brief, for my short date of breath
    Is not so long as is a tedious tale.
    Romeo, there dead, was husband to that Juliet,   240
    And she, there dead, that's Romeo's faithful wife.
    I married them, and their stol'n marriage day
    Was Tybalt's doomsday, whose untimely death
    Banished the new-made bridegroom from the city,

247: **perforce:** by force

254: **wrought:** worked

255: **form:** external appearance

258: **being:** before

260: **stayed:** held back, prevented

262: **prefixed:** appointed beforehand (i.e., pre-fixed)

266: **ere:** before

267: **untimely:** before (their) natural time

275: **privy:** in on the secret, aware

275: **aught:** anything

276: **miscarried by my fault:** i.e., failed because of my actions

For whom, and not for Tybalt, Juliet pined.   245
You, to remove that siege of grief from her,
Betrothed and would have married her perforce
To County Paris. Then comes she to me,
And, with wild looks, bid me devise some mean
To rid her from this second marriage,   250
Or in my cell there would she kill herself.
Then gave I her, so tutored by my art,
A sleeping potion, which so took effect
As I intended, for it wrought on her
The form of death. Meantime, I writ to Romeo,   255
That he should hither come as this dire night,
To help to take her from her borrowed grave,
Being the time the potion's force should cease.
But he which bore my letter, Friar John,
Was stayed by accident and yesternight   260
Returned my letter back. Then all alone
At the prefixed hour of her waking,
Came I to take her from her kindred's vault,
Meaning to keep her closely at my cell,
Till I conveniently could send to Romeo.   265
But when I came, some minute ere the time
Of her awakening, here untimely lay
The noble Paris and true Romeo dead.
She wakes, and I entreated her come forth,
And bear this work of heaven with patience,   270
But then a noise did scare me from the tomb,
And she, too desperate, would not go with me,
But, as it seems, did violence on herself.
All this I know, and to the marriage
Her nurse is privy. And if aught in this   275
Miscarried by my fault, let my old life
Be sacrificed some hour before his time,
Unto the rigour of severest law.

PRINCE
We have known thee for a holy man.
Where's Romeo's man? What can he say to this?   280

286: **I departed not:** If I departed not

288: **raised the watch:** i.e., alerted the guard

289: **what made your master:** what was your master doing

303: **winking:** turning a blind eye

304: **a brace:** a couple

Line 305: "O brother Montague, give me thy hand": David Sabin as Montague and Edward Gero as Capulet in The Shakespeare Theatre's 2001-2002 production directed by Rachael Kavanaugh

Photo: Carol Rosegg

306: **jointure:** estate settled on a woman upon her husband's death

BALTHASAR

I brought my master news of Juliet's death,
And then in post he came from Mantua
To this same place, to this same monument.
This letter he early bid me give his father,
And threatened me with death, going in the vault,   285
If I departed not and left him there.

PRINCE

Give me the letter; I will look on it. —
Where is the county's page that raised the watch? —
Sirrah, what made your master in this place?

PAGE

He came with flowers to strew his lady's grave,   290
And bid me stand aloof, and so I did.
Anon comes one with light to ope the tomb,
And by and by my master drew on him,
And then I ran away to call the watch.

PRINCE

This letter doth make good the friar's words,   295
Their course of love, the tidings of her death.
And here he writes that he did buy a poison
Of a poor 'pothecary, and therewithal
Came to this vault to die and lie with Juliet.
Where be these enemies? Capulet! Montague!   300
See, what a scourge is laid upon your hate,
That heaven finds means to kill your joys with love.
And I for winking at your discords too
Have lost a brace of kinsmen. All are punished.

CAPULET

O brother Montague, give me thy hand.   305
This is my daughter's jointure, for no more
Can I demand.

MONTAGUE

     But I can give thee more,
For I will raise her statue in pure gold

311: **rate:** estimation, value

314: **poor:** unhappy

315: **glooming:** cloudy, dismal

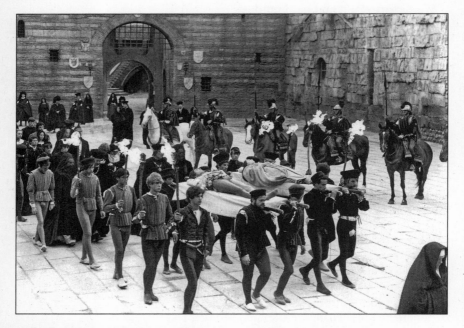

Zeffirelli added a funeral scene for Romeo and Juliet in his 1968 movie production that was not originally in Shakespeare's text

Courtesy: Douglas Lanier

That while Verona by that name is known.   310
There shall no figure at such rate be set
As that of true and faithful Juliet.

CAPULET
As rich shall Romeo's by his lady's lie.
Poor sacrifices of our enmity!

PRINCE
A glooming peace this morning with it brings.   315
The sun, for sorrow, will not show his head.
Go hence, to have more talk of these sad things.
Some shall be pardoned and some punished,
For never was a story of more woe
Than this of Juliet and her Romeo.   320

[Exeunt]

The Cast Speaks

Marie Macaisa

In the text of the play, directors, actors, and other interpreters of Shakespeare's work find a wealth of information. A hallmark of Shakespeare's writing is to tell us more than we need to know about a particular character, more than is needed to understand the plot. For example, in Iago, we are presented with a myriad of motivations for him to destroy Othello and Desdemona's marriage. Janet Suzman, director of the acclaimed 1987 Johannesburg *Othello*, offers the following: "He's jealous of Cassio's advancement; he's suspicious that the Moor has had a fling with his wife Emilia; he despises Othello because he's black or because he's credulous; he's disgusted with Desdemona for breaking the rules of white Venice." Yet, despite the spate of reasons, we remain very much uncertain of his primary motivation, an uncertainty that Shakespeare reinforces with Iago's response to Othello's direct question: "Demand me nothing: what you know, you know: / From this time forth I never will speak word."

While providing extra information, Shakespeare (like all playwrights and unlike novelists) also leaves gaps. We are thus coaxed to fill in the missing information ourselves, either through reasonable surmises (we can guess that Gertrude and Claudius were attracted to each other before Old Hamlet died) or through back stories we supply on our own (the idea that Mercutio was disappointed in love, not present in the text, to explain his attitude). This mix, simultaneously knowing too much and not enough about the characters, enables us to paint vivid, varied interpretations of the same play.

In staging a play, directors create a vision for their production starting from the text but also moving beyond it, by making decisions on what *isn't* in the text. In collaboration with actors, they flesh out the characters: they discuss what they might be like, they create stories that explain their actions, they determine motivations, and they speculate on the nature of their relationships. In Shakespeare they have a rich text to draw on and hundreds of years of performances for inspiration. Thus we, the audience, can experience a play anew each time we see a different production: perhaps it is in an unfamiliar setting, perhaps it is in a scene or characterization we hadn't noticed in the past, perhaps it is in the realization that we somehow sympathize with different characters now (for example, the parents Lord and Lady Capulet instead of the teenage lovers Romeo and Juliet). Whatever the case, a closer look into one cast's interpretation creates an opportunity for us to make up our own minds about their stories and in the process, gain new insights not just into a play hundreds of years old but, quite possibly, ourselves.

CHICAGO SHAKESPEARE THEATER, 2005

"The Chicago Shakespeare Theater's 2005 production of *Romeo and Juliet*," says director Mark Lamos, "is a play about lightness that is overtaken by panic and darkness. You have the vigor of Mercutio, the bawdy humor of the nurse, and the lightness, unmatchable buoyancy of Juliet." Throughout the play, moments of lightness and darkness are juxtaposed as Romeo and Juliet begin to understand that their lives are ruled by nature and by fate. "In this remarkable young couple," Lamos adds, "Shakespeare has given us two teenagers who are more adult than the adults in their world; they are, in fact, Renaissance humanists in a corrupt and violent world." Even as they revel in their meeting and then their love, Friar Laurence cautions, "Violent delights have violent ends," and the play hurtles towards tragedy at light-speed. Professor Peter Holland observes that little in this play is ever "in time"; this is the great drama about being short of time, out of time, never timely.

Most of these cast interviews were conducted in March, 2005, during tech week. (Tech week is the most crucial week of the preproduction portion of the show. It is generally the first time the participants are at the theater with the full set, costumes, and orchestra. The lighting, sound, and stage cues are being set at this time.) The actors were interviewed individually and asked about their characters, their main relationships, and a scene or two in which their character figures. Keep in mind that these interviews represent but one interpretation of the play. You may be surprised, you may agree or disagree strongly with a point of view. That is exactly the point.

THE HOUSE OF MONTAGUE
Lord and Lady Montague: David Lively and Susan Wands

The Montagues, according to the actors who play them, come from old money and are a little more formally educated than the Capulets, who are noveau-riche. Consequently, they are more reserved. Romeo is as much a mystery to them as Juliet is to the Capulets, yet they are shown making the effort to understand him. After the opening fight, Montague tells Benvolio of Romeo's early morning teary wanderings but confesses to not knowing why: "I neither know it nor can learn of him." Lady Montague expresses relief that Romeo was not part of the fight: "Right glad I am he was not at this fray." Neverthe-less, the Montagues scarcely appear in the play (especially compared to the Capulets) and the actors wondered why. They concluded that they were meant to be seen through Romeo's eyes.

David Lively: When Montague first comes on, you get a sense of where Romeo gets his love of language and poetry. Montague is the first one to talk in that poetic way:

> Many a morning hath he there been seen,
> With tears augmenting the fresh morning dew.
> Adding to clouds more clouds with his deep sighs;

It's very Romeo-like, and you get a sense of Romeo's upbringing. I get the feeling that he and his wife still care very much for each other and are genuinely still in love.

I have a brief moment in the spotlight in the last scene of the play. Montague is the last one to come onstage and he's all alone. Nobody but him knows about Lady Montague's passing and he delivers a few short but powerful lines showing his grief. The words he uses are very telling, I think: "O thou untaught! what manners is in this? / To press before thy father to a grave?"

Alluding to "manners" at this time hints that they were very proper people and raised Romeo to be the same way. There is anger in his grief, but he accepts Capulet's hand extended in peace. He does talk about raising her statue in gold after Capulet offers Juliet's estate, almost like merchants outdoing each other. But you can't leave the audience with that, so he has to be sincere.

Susan Wands: I don't think Lady Montague had a healthy relationship with her son. Women then had to live through the arranged marriages of their children. I think her own marriage was one based on social status. We're conjecturing (and this isn't in the text) that part of the feud arose originally because Capulet possibly wanted to marry Lady Montague and when that didn't work, he married his present Lady Capulet. Her death is one of the things that put the feud to rest.

Lady Montague is one of the smallest speaking roles in the play, and she disappears after the disappearance of Romeo. You learn at the end that she killed herself. You might be tempted to ask, "Why didn't she just go find him?" But families then were so caught up in social status and marrying their children off for advantageous reasons; when it's clear that her son will not be successful living in Verona, she felt she had no choice but to kill herself.

Romeo, their son: Carman Lacivita

I think of Romeo as a typical teenager. He wants to hide from everything, he shuts himself in his room, and he likes to be in the dark. He thinks he's found love with Rosaline but he enjoys being away from her because he revels in the darkness. However, he discovers light when he sees Juliet—"What light through yonder window breaks?" I think he discovers love when he discovers light and vice-versa. He realizes he was infatuated with Rosaline and it was just a crush. When he meets Juliet, he asks, "Did my heart love till now?"

Mercutio is like an older brother to Romeo. He's the one who has been through it all, has experienced it all. Romeo goes to him for intellectual sparring. When they're sparring, no one else gets it. It's similar with Juliet. When he talks to her, his language is lifted. He's elevated intellectually by both of them. Regarding the bawdiness in my exchanges with Mercutio, we definitely go there in this production. The relationship that Robert [Petkoff, the actor playing Mercutio] and I worked out is that we're comfortable doing this, but it doesn't mean anything will happen. This is just the way boys play with each other.

The Friar is his father figure. Romeo's language to him shows reverence and respect. He only mentions his own father twice in the play, once at the end when he asks Balthasar, "Is my father well?" There's no intimation in the text that I'm mad at him or estranged, but that relationship isn't all that developed. I think Romeo is much more inclined towards his mother.

There are many important scenes for Romeo but the scene with the greatest expectation is the balcony scene. Everyone knows that scene. What I try

Robert Petkoff as Mercutio, Carman Lacivita as Romeo, and Brian Hamman as Benvolio
Photo: Liz Lauren

to do is to live that experience such that it is my one last chance at real true love. That's a huge but good obstacle. I know if I'm going towards that, my need will be stronger. It helps that she's far, far above me and I can't reach her. That strengthens the need even more. Shakespeare's language allows for that—I have to reach her with words. I've found that the way he's written it makes you keep thinking about what else you need to say to keep her there as long as possible. She can go inside at any time.

Mercutio, kinsman to the Prince and friend to Romeo: Robert Petkoff

I believe Mercutio is the anti-Romeo. I think he is someone who has been stepped on romantically, has lost in love, and has therefore turned completely against it. There is nothing in the text that says this, but his view of love is so anti-romantic, something must have caused it.

He says these interesting lines, "Give me a case to put my visage in: / A visor for a visor! what care I / What curious eye doth quote deformities?" To me that means he doesn't think of himself as handsome; he's deformed in some way. It doesn't necessarily have to be a physical disfigurement, simply that his appeal to women is limited. Every reference he makes to love is about women as whores, as objects of lust but not love. His advice to Romeo is "If love be rough with you, be rough with love; / Prick love for pricking, and you beat love down." It's very adolescent, not very mature.

He is very disdainful of Tybalt. That stems from the fact that they are both soldiers, and Tybalt is known for his new form of fighting: the proper form. Mercutio, however, has been in the battlefield and knows that the young men around him who followed those rules died quickly. He sees that everyone holds Tybalt in high regard as a swordsman but to him, it's all show. So when he does encounter Tybalt, he has no patience for him. It's incomprehensible to him that he's going to die because of Tybalt.

Mercutio has an opinion as to what Romeo should be like and he pushes him to be that: "Now art thou what thou art, by art as well as by nature." They are intellectual equals. He bandies a bit with Benvolio but it's always short and flat, whereas he has long speeches with Romeo full of layers of meanings and double entendres. There is a lot of homoeroticism underlying it, but it doesn't have to be classified. In this case, it's purposely ambivalent; we're not playing that up. If Mercutio has the desire to spend time with Romeo, it isn't to have sex with him. It's to have that sublime companionship that he can't seem to find anywhere else. And—until Romeo found Rosaline and then Juliet—Romeo couldn't find either. It was the perfect friendship.

Mercutio is a great wit. The Queen Mab speech is an example, but that's so much more. He talks about fantastical things and the effect Queen Mab has on people. He makes you believe that he believes in that himself. But then he devolves and the speech does as well, to a very base evaluation of what human beings want in their dream world. When he gets to the part about "Sometime she driveth o'er a soldier's neck," having been a soldier, the experiences catch up with him again. Suddenly he's talking about the people he's been with and it takes him to a deeper, scarier place. From then on, it becomes very upsetting. This speech is the key to revealing, and setting up, who he is. At the end, he's on top of Romeo, holding him down, and you're not sure whether he's in a fevered state of mind or in control. The name "Mercutio" suggests mercurial, and I want people to not know where they stand with him.

Benvolio, nephew to Montague and friend to Romeo: Brian Hamman

Benvolio is Romeo's cousin and friends with Mercutio. I think Romeo introduced them to each other, though he (Benvolio) is not as close to Mercutio as Romeo is. His friendship with Romeo is also different from Mercutio's friendship with Romeo. I play him in the middle—he's a lover but not as much as Romeo, and he'll fight but he won't get as agitated as Mercutio.

Benvolio is the peacemaker and is the most even-tempered of everyone in the play. He's the person who's always called upon to explain what happened; you know you can always get a straight answer from him. He describes everyone truthfully: Tybalt is fiery, Mercutio is bold and brave, and he asks the right questions of Romeo such that you (and he) can see his heart.

When he hears about the ball, he wants to go and convinces Romeo to do the same. There is no fear of going to the party, no fear of trouble or losing his life. He wants Romeo to attend so he can see all these beautiful women and forget all about Rosaline, who is causing Romeo much woe. He's so convinced they should just go and have fun and nothing will come of it.

Why does he feel that? He's of a younger generation; the feud itself doesn't really mean much to him. He wants to see it end and he's more than willing to express that and even fight his own guys to do so. Maybe the feud is dying down.

I don't agree that Benvolio can't fight. He's fully capable of it and he runs into the melee. But he drops his sword and tries to stop the fight. His function is to set up the fear of Tybalt, one of the most critical characters in the play. It is Tybalt's need to keep the feud going that sets up the second half. In that scene we are trying to show the contrast between Benvolio's calm, peaceful nature and Tybalt's fieriness.

THE HOUSE OF CAPULET
Lord and Lady Capulet: Steve Hendrickson and Susan Hart

The actors playing Lord and Lady Capulet see these parents as well-intentioned people who want only the best for their daughter. As heads of a well-to-do family, each parent was kept busy by responsibilities: he with the business and she with running the household. They probably didn't spend much time with their daughter and didn't know her well; this was not unusual in those times. They both believe that the best thing they can do for their daughter is to ensure that she marries well. They rejoice when Paris declares his interest, for they know they can't do any better than him: he is wealthy, handsome, kind, and really seems to love Juliet. When Juliet wants no part of the marriage, when she is disobedient for no apparent reason, they react in a very human way.

Steve Hendrickson: What makes this play so powerful is that everybody is trying to help and make things better in their way, and the harder they try, the worse things become.

As much as the Capulets want the match with Paris to happen, they are not in a hurry to marry their daughter off. In the first scene with Paris, Capulet tells him that his daughter is really young and that perhaps they should wait a couple of years ("Let two more summers wither in their pride, / Ere we may think her ripe to be a bride."). Also, it's very important to him that Juliet like Paris. He encourages Paris to meet her at the party, get to know her. He takes her feelings into account, which is a very radical thing for that age. Young girls, they were supposed to be treated as property.

As the play progresses, however, that point of view takes over. He was really angry with Juliet when she turns down the marriage (Act 3, Scene 5) but it's important to remember what else was going on. His family has been riven by stress. Tybalt's dead and we know other children have died (Act 1, Scene 2, Line 14: "The earth has swallow'd all my hopes but she"), there is a suggestion that Paris is losing interest or may not be willing to wait anymore. For the parents, there's a sense that their world is starting to unravel and that this marriage is the way to set things right again. So even then, it's a positive but misbegotten attempt to set things right. They truly believe that if she gets married, she'll be happy. Then, when she says no... In a different time under different circumstances, there might not have been as big a reaction, but she says no at just the wrong time and Capulet just erupts and reverts to his traditional role.

He and Lady Capulet have been married for a number of years, and the ardor has cooled a bit. Even if Lady Capulet hasn't actually had an affair, she certainly casts her eye about on the younger men at the party. Perhaps Capulet has a thing for the younger women as well (though this isn't in the text.) They have had other children, but Juliet is the only one left and they think of Tybalt as their son. When Capulet turns on Tybalt at the party and berates him publicly, what I'm trying to impart is "my son is dead and you're all that's left so stop screwing up. Be better. Be more responsible." The older members of the families are tired at this point. They may have been vigorous participants in the feud in their youth, but they're not young anymore, and they would just as soon have it stop.

Susan Hart as Lady Capulet with ensemble
Photo: Liz Lauren

Susan Hart: We explored what it meant for her to be a woman of her times. I don't think of her as unfeeling or unloving; she's not a bad person. In fact, she stands up to Capulet when she sees him getting angrier and angrier at Juliet. She gets between them and tells him, "You are too hot." However she only goes so far; she knows her duty, and her powers were very limited then.

She probably hasn't slept much since Tybalt died, and the family is in deep mourning for him, especially her. There's a subtle suggestion that something might have have been going on between them and at one point, Capulet does give her a questioning look, but then again, he's an old drunk.

I love the scene between her and Juliet about avenging Tybalt's death. She tells Juliet not to worry, she knows someone in Mantua and she can have Romeo poisoned. Rich, Italian women did that at that time! She was an Italian diva; they had resources.

I think she loves Juliet very much and is devastated when she dies:

> But one, poor one, one poor and loving child,
> But one thing to rejoice and solace in,
> And cruel death hath catch'd it from my sight!

As people, the Capulets can't be all that bad. They have a blabbermouth on staff, a wet nurse who's still there after fourteen years, who feels comfortable standing up to Capulet. They can't be hateful people. The Nurse is a great comfort and relief to her, and they both care very much about her daughter, her little girl.

Juliet, their daughter: Julia Coffey

Juliet is the Capulets' only child (Capulet says, "The earth hath swallow'd all my hopes but she"). As the only daughter, they have to get her married and married well. However, marriage was dangerous for young women then, so her father was trying to get Paris to delay the ceremony ("Let two more summers wither in their pride, / Ere we may think her ripe to be a bride"). Maybe he knows from experience—his young wife having had so many miscarriages and dead babies. The possibility of Juliet dying in childbirth was great, and she is their only hope for passing on their genes and securing their position in the world.

Juliet is very isolated in life. She's never out by herself, she always has a guard with her because of the violent street fighting between the Capulets and Montagues. The only places she goes to are her bedroom, the atrium of the castle, maybe a couple of parties in her own castle, and church. That's it. Fortunately she's educated because she is of a certain class. Why else can she say these amazing words? She's not given an opportunity to voice her mind to anybody until she meets Romeo; it's in meeting him that she finds herself. The sonnet when they first meet (Act 1, Scene 5, Lines 95-108) is outstanding.

What a lot of people conclude about Romeo's attraction to Rosaline is that he's changeable and therefore the love he feels for Juliet is cheapened, but it's not the case. He's connecting with that romantic need in him and the desire

Julia Coffey as Juliet and Rondi Reed as the Nurse
Photo: Liz Lauren

to find somebody. This enables him when he does meet Juliet to be open to the possibility. This also stems in part from his family. Romeo's family is very loving towards him. In Juliet's household, however, there's tension. We know her father is tyrannical and has a temper, and she's not close to her own mother. Her mother figure is the Nurse, who loves her, but in a limited way. She's bawdy, uneducated, and is of an inferior class. I don't think, as well-meaning as her parents are, that they love her the way the Montagues love Romeo.

Perhaps she could have told her parents after the ball about Romeo. But she's so distant from them and has nobody to talk to except the Nurse, who's not really in a position to take up her cause. If they had just a second to breathe (but they don't), they could have realized that maybe Rosaline is a Capulet too, this feud is petering out, Romeo has a good relationship with his parents, and he could have gone to them and told them he was in love with Juliet and could we work this out. All these missed opportunities and that's the real drama. People have good intentions, and they think they're helping but all they're doing is overcomplicating matters and making it worse. Juliet does that too by not going to her parents.

One of her most important scenes is Act 3, Scene 5, where she cuts the bond with Nurse. She comes to the realization that not only has she grown apart, she has a future that's going to be completely different from the woman who has raised her. The Nurse can't help her anymore. Further, she has turned against Juliet by suggesting she marry Paris. She realizes then that she's on her own, an adult, all alone. The last person who might be able to help is the Friar, and she decides that if that doesn't work, she's going to kill herself.

> Go counselor;
> Thou and my bosom henceforth shall be twain.
> I'll to the friar, to know his remedy:
> If all else fail, myself have power to die.

Paris, Juliet's suitor, kinsman to the prince: John Hoogenakker

Paris is a young aristocrat, a nobleman. He's kin to the Prince and is distantly related to Mercutio. (Romeo refers to him as "Mercutio's kinsman, noble County Paris!") We're playing with the idea that the Prince has set up Paris and Juliet—the Prince suggested the match to Paris, who brings it up to Capulet, who's very excited. There will be interaction at the ball, though no lines to support any of that.

He strikes me as someone who's not a bad guy, but he might be a little shallow. Maybe he had a nice collection of stamps or something, but there's no flash there. If Juliet was imagining marriage with him, it wouldn't be full of love or passion. But she would be comfortable and both families would gain.

There is a scene where he's talking to Friar Laurence (Act 4, Scene 1) and then this girl comes in, her face wet with tears, and she's unbearably sad. He assumes it's because she's lost her cousin, and his heart goes out to her. She has a spirit that he doesn't really understand and is very attractive to him at that time.

I believe there's a lot of text to support that Paris really feels deeply for Juliet and cares for her: the fact that he goes to grieve at her grave without being asked; the fact that when he happens upon the guy he blames for all the problems, he tries to have him arrested. It is possible to interpret that Paris is only in this match for reasons of financial gain. We ultimately decided he was a good guy instead of a heel, so we've taken away some of the text that might suggest he's only in it for the money. However he also doesn't die in this production, so none of this is shown and the audience can legitimately wonder.

Tybalt, nephew to Lady Capulet: Michael Polak

Tybalt is Juliet's cousin (although "cousin" was a looser term back then). His father was Lady Capulet's brother, though you never hear about his parents. You don't know what happened to them, what befell them.

He can be considered as the antagonist. He kills Mercutio; he can't let go of the feud. They set him up as the swordsman of the town; he's not afraid to use swords when words aren't enough. Most of the time in the scenes, he seems to be fiery and upset. Even at the Capulet's ball, though he sees that it's great and people are having a good time, when he spots people who shouldn't be there, he feels he has to do something. He doesn't care if he disrupts the party and possibly hurts someone. He doesn't at all think it would be a sin to kill a Monague there.

When he dies, he is mourned by the grief-stricken Capulets. To them, he was a wonderful, loyal, family person. A lot of times, productions have insinuated that there's been a sexual relationship between Lady Capulet and Tybalt. Certainly Capulet's response doesn't seem to be the same as Lady Capulet, Juliet, or even the Nurse. The last time they spoke was in anger, when Capulet shamed him in front of the whole party, and I expected him to be more upset and remorseful. But who knows.

Nurse to Juliet: Rondi Reed

The Nurse is of the earth, practical, not the brightest, but she's probably not been educated. She can't read but she's smart in some ways, crafty in others. She doesn't have the ability of the Friar to look at the big picture. When she runs to him to find Romeo, he is organized and clear-thinking, and he tells her it will all be fine. She doesn't possess that facility; however, she's very good at improvising and dealing with problems that are obvious and right in front of her. She runs the other servants and organizes the household.

She speaks of her husband fondly; he "was a merry man!" She had a daughter, Susan, who was the same age as Juliet, and then when she lost her and her husband passed away, the Capulets have been like family to her. She was a wet nurse to Juliet, who lived with them at least till she was weaned, as was the custom then. She has an almost grandmotherly relationship to Juliet. She's able to talk to her, teach her things, say things to her that her mother doesn't. At one point, Lady Capulet asks her to leave so she can talk to her daughter in private, but she gets called back immediately:

> Nurse, give leave awhile,
> We must talk in secret:—nurse, come back again;
> I have remember'd me, thou's hear our counsel.

An important turning point for the Nurse is Act 3, Scene 2, when the Nurse tells Juliet about Tybalt's death and that Romeo slew him. She's cursing and railing at him, and Juliet wins her back with her love of Romeo. Juliet is disconsolate, and the Nurse takes a pause and then says, "I'll find Romeo to comfort you: / I wot [know] well where he is." That's important. She's not only sneaking off to the marketplace, she's doing something against the law, because Romeo is a fugitive. It flies in the face of the Prince's law, the Capulets' will, and her own feeling about Tybalt's death. Tybalt was very important to her. But her love for Juliet is that great.

When Capulet blows up and threatens to throw Juliet out of the house (Act 3, Scene 5), the Nurse thinks it's too much. It's all too much. So she assesses the situation and tells Juliet how it is: Romeo's gone, he's of no use to you, it's best to let that go. All things considered, it might be best, she advises Juliet, if she "married with the county." It's that practicality again.

However, Juliet sees that as a big betrayal; she thought that the Nurse understood how deeply she felt for Romeo. It is then that Juliet decides to cut the Nurse out of her life.

Peter, servant to Juliet's nurse: Danny Rhodes

Peter is the Capulets' servant and the Nurse's man. He has a good relationship with the nurse. In this production, I get an important scene: I accidentally invite Romeo to the Capulet ball. My master has given me a list of people to invite but I can't read, and I ask for his (Romeo's) help. Then I say, "if you be not of the house of Montagues, I pray, come and crush a cup of wine." That scene is not always played by Peter; the text just says "Servant." It's a very comedic scene and I enjoy that. I contribute to the comedy as well in the scenes with Mercutio and the Nurse.

OTHER CITIZENS

Escalus, Prince of Verona: Nick Sandys

The actor playing the Prince also plays the Apothecary. Thus he gets to be the characters that are of the highest and the lowest stature in the play.

The Prince comes in at the beginning, middle, and end, and there is almost a choric structure to his speeches. He is very formal and his language reflects that. He bears a lot of responsibility for the way the events unfolded. Not only did he banish Romeo, he also could have stopped the feud earlier but he didn't. He might have escalated it, in fact, by meeting with each party separately and ordering them to stop instead of meeting with them together and dealing with the issues. He was probably quite exasperated at these fights pulling him away from whatever business he was involved in. He's shocked and upset at the end because he feels responsible for the deaths and also because has lost his kinsman Mercutio and (in the text) Paris:

> And I for winking at your discords too
> Have lost a brace of kinsmen: all are punish'd.

However, Paris didn't die in this production, so we changed "brace of" to "noble." He still has more than enough reason to grieve.

Friar Laurence: Mike Nussbaum

The Friar is the confessor and father figure to Romeo. Romeo has come to him with his problems rather than his father. He means well; he tries to help,

Mike Nussbaum as Friar Laurence
Photo: Liz Lauren

but as he says, "A greater power than we can contradict / Hath thwarted our intents." In a sense he is the reason why this thing has turned into a tragedy, but he does it out of the best of intentions.

On the other hand, he does things that he has no right to do, like marrying this young couple without the approval of their parents, without the posting of the banns. Not only that, since it may not be a legal marriage until there's consummation, he even arranges for that before he sends Romeo to Mantua. He tells Romeo, "Tybalt would kill thee, / But thou slew'st Tybalt; there are thou happy [fortunate] too." How can he countenance murder, even in self-defense? But he does. In many ways, he's complicit morally if not criminally.

Why does he do this? I think he's fond of Romeo but also of scheming. He's a man who loves to see himself spinning webs and being at the center of things. He spends so much time in the gardens, and he's almost like an alchemist, studying herbs and plants and their effects. When he's presented with a real-world problem, his solution involves his herbs though, he can't know for sure they will work exactly as he thinks. He tells Juliet, "Thou shalt continue two and forty hours, / And then awake as from a pleasant sleep." I can't believe he knows that exactly. As an actor I'm going to experiment with how many hours I think she'll actually be asleep. He's taking a chance!

What if she wakes up an hour before they get there and finds herself in the tomb, all alone, in the dark? What a frightening thing. What if she wakes up an hour later, and they're all there and the whole thing could fall apart too? The Friar is taking a big chance. Anybody who takes a chance like that is culpable. He runs away at the end—a noise frightens him. This is another terrible failing on his part. He leaves her there for fear he'll get caught. He's far from guiltless.

Friar John: David Lively

Friar John reinforces the theme that things happening by accident, even if you try to steer them in the right direction. We get a vocal response from the audience, we hear people react audibly when he tells Friar Laurence that the plague kept him from getting the letter delivered. The director and I made the choice that Friar John does not know the importance of the mission so he does not realize what is at stake. He sees Friar Laurence react to his news and only then does make the expected response. Otherwise he didn't know what the big deal was.

Apothecary: Nick Sandys

The Apothecary is the poorest person, and I think of him as a merchant who's failed in business. I describe the voice I produce for him as "gargling with gravel." It's supposed to hint at the death rattle. We wanted him to represent the darker, sinister counterpart of Friar Laurence. While the Friar's potion puts you in a deep sleep resembling death, his actually kills you. We dressed him in robes vaguely resembling the Friar's and kept him in the shadows. He utters only seven lines, but he is talked about and described by Romeo before he even comes on stage.

A Voice Coach's Perspective on Speaking Shakespeare

KEEPING SHAKESPEARE PRACTICAL

Andrew Wade

Andrew Wade with members of the Guthrie Experience for Actors in Training

Why, you might be wondering, is it so important to keep Shakespeare practical? What do I mean by practical? Why is this the way to discover how to speak the text and understand it?

Plays themselves are not simply literary events—they demand interpreters in the deepest sense of the word, and the language of Shakespeare requires, therefore, not a vocal demonstration of writing techniques but an imaginative response to that writing. The key word here is imagination. The task of the voice coach is to offer relevant choices to the actor so that the actor's imagination is titillated, excited by the language, which he or she can then share with an audience, playing on that audience's imagination. Take the word "IF"—it is only composed of two letters when written, but if you say it aloud and listen to what it implies, then your reaction, the way the word plays through you, can change the perception of meaning. "Ifffffffff"... you might hear and feel it implying "possibilities," "choices," "questioning," "trying to work something out." The saying of this word provokes active investigation of thought. What an apt word to launch a play: "If music be the food of love, play on" (Act 1, Scene 1 in *Twelfth Night, or What You Will*). How this word engages the listener and immediately sets up an involvement is about more than audibility.

How we verbalize sounds has a direct link to meaning and understanding. In the words of Touchstone in *As You Like It,* "Much virtue in if."

I was working with a company in Vancouver on *Macbeth,* and at the end of the first week's rehearsal—after having explored our voices and opening out different pieces of text to hear the possibilities of the rhythm, feeling how the meter affects the thinking and feeling, looking at structure and form— one of the actors admitted he was also a writer of soap operas and that I had completely changed his way of writing. Specifically, in saying a line like, "The multitudinous seas incarnadine / Making the green one red" he heard the complexity of meaning revealed in the use of polysyllabic words becoming monosyllabic, layered upon the words' individual dictionary definitions. The writer was reminded that merely reproducing the speech of everyday life was nowhere near as powerful and effective as language that is shaped.

Do you think soap operas would benefit from rhyming couplets? Somehow this is difficult to imagine! But, the writer's comments set me thinking. As I am constantly trying to find ways of exploring the acting process, of opening out actors' connection with language that isn't their own, I thought it would be a good idea to involve writers and actors in some practical work on language. After talking to Cicely Berry (Voice Director, the Royal Shakespeare Company) and Colin Chambers (the then RSC Production Adviser), we put together a group of writers and actors who were interested in taking part. It was a fascinating experience all round, and it broke down barriers and misconceptions.

The actors discovered, for instance, that a writer is not coming from a very different place as they are in their creative search; that an idea or an image may result from a struggle to define a gut feeling and not from some crafted, well-formed idea in the head. The physical connection of language to the body was reaffirmed. After working with a group on Yeats' poem, *Easter 1916,* Ann Devlin changed the title of the play she was writing for the Royal Shakespeare Company to *After Easter.* She had experienced the poem read aloud by a circle of participants, each voice becoming a realization of the shape of the writing. Thus it made a much fuller impact on her and caused her thinking to shift. Such practical exchanges, through language work and voice, feed and stimulate my work to go beyond making sure the actors' voices are technically sound.

It is, of course, no different when we work on a Shakespeare play. A similar connection with the language is crucial. Playing Shakespeare, in many ways, is crafted instinct. The task is thus to find the best way to tap into someone's imagination. As Peter Brook put it: "People forget that a text is dumb. To make it speak, one must create a communication machine. A living network, like a nervous system, must be made if a text which comes from far away is to touch the sensibility of the present."

This journey is never to be taken for granted. It is the process that every text must undergo every time it is staged. There is no definitive rehearsal that would solve problems or indicate ways of staging a given play. Again, this is where creative, practical work on voice can help forge new meaning by offering areas of exploration and challenge. The central idea behind my work comes back to posing the question, "How does meaning change by speaking out aloud?" It would be unwise to jump hastily to the end process for, as Peter Brook says, "Shakespeare's words are records of the words that he wanted spoken, words issuing from people's mouths, with pitch, pause and rhythm and gesture as part of their meaning. A word does not start as a word—it is the end product which begins as an impulse, stimulated by attitude and behavior which dictates the need for expression." (1)

PRACTICALLY SPEAKING

Something happens when we vocalize, when we isolate sounds, when we start to speak words aloud, when we put them to the test of our physicality, of our anatomy. We expose ourselves in a way that makes taking the language back more difficult. Our body begins a debate with itself, becomes alive with the vibrations of sound produced in the mouth or rooted deep in the muscles that aim at defining sound. In fact, the spoken words bring into play all the senses, before sense and another level of meaning are reached.

"How do I know what I think, until I see what I say," Oscar Wilde once said. A concrete illustration of this phrase was reported to me when I was leading a workshop recently. A grandmother said the work we had done that day reminded her of what her six-year-old grandson had said to his mother while they were driving through Wales: "Look, mummy, sheep! Sheep! Sheep!" "You don't have to keep telling us," the mother replied, but the boy said, "How do I know they're there, if I don't tell you?!"

Therefore, when we speak of ideas, of sense, we slightly take for granted those physical processes which affect and change their meaning. We tend to separate something that is an organic whole. In doing so, we become blind to the fact that it is precisely this physical connection to the words that enables the actors to make the language theirs.

The struggle for meaning is not just impressionistic theater mystique; it is an indispensable aspect of the rehearsal process and carries on during the life of every production. In this struggle, practical work on Shakespeare is vital and may help spark creativity and shed some light on the way meaning is born into language. After a performance of *More Words*, a show devised and directed by Cicely Berry and myself, Katie Mitchell (a former Artistic Director of The Other Place in Stratford-upon-Avon) gave me an essay by Ted Hughes that echoes with the piece. In it, Ted Hughes compares the writing of a poem—the coming into existence of words—to the capture of a wild animal. You will notice that in the following passage Hughes talks of "spirit" or "living parts" but never of "thought" or "sense." With great care and precaution, he advises, "It is better to call (the poem) an assembly of living parts moved by a single spirit. The living parts are the words, the images, the rhythms. The spirit is the life which inhabits them when they all work together. It is impossible to say which comes first, parts or spirit."

This is also true of life in words, as many are connected directly to one or several of our senses. Here Hughes talks revealingly of "the five senses," of "word," "action," and "muscle," all things which a practical approach to language is more likely to allow one to perceive and do justice to.

Words that live are those which we hear, like "click" or "chuckle," or which we see, like "freckled" or "veined," or which we taste, like "vinegar" or "sugar," or touch, like "prickle" or "oily," or smell, like "tar" or "onion," words which belong to one of the five senses. Or words that act and seem to use their muscles, like "flick" or "balance." (2)

In this way, practically working on Shakespeare to arrive at understanding lends itself rather well, I think, to what Adrian Noble (former Artistic Director of the RSC) calls "a theater of poetry." a form of art that, rooted deeply in its classical origins, would seek to awaken the imagination of its audiences through love and respect for words while satisfying our eternal craving for myths and twice-told tales.

This can only be achieved at some cost. There is indeed a difficult battle to fight and hopefully win "the battle of the word to survive." This phrase was coined by Michael Redgrave at the beginning of the 1950s, a period when theater began to be deeply influenced by more physical forms, such as mime. (3) Although the context is obviously different, the fight today is of the same nature.

LISTENING TO SHAKESPEARE

Because of the influence of television, our way of speaking as well as listening has changed. It is crucial to be aware of this. We can get fairly close to the way *Henry V* or *Hamlet* was staged in Shakespeare's time, we can try also to reconstruct the way English was spoken. But somehow, all these fall short of the real and most important goal: the Elizabethan ear. How did one "hear" a Shakespeare play? This is hardest to know. My personal view is that we will probably never know for sure. We are, even when we hear a Shakespeare play or a recording from the past, bound irrevocably to modernity. The Elizabethan ear was no doubt different from our own, as people were not spoken to or entertained in the same way. A modern voice has to engage us in a different way in order to make us truly listen in a society that seems to rely solely on the belief that image is truth, that it is more important to show rather than to tell.

Sometimes, we say that a speech in Shakespeare, or even an entire production, is not well-spoken, not up to standard. What do we mean by that? Evidently, there are a certain number of "guidelines" that any actor now has to know when working on a classical text. Yet, even when these are known, actors still have to make choices when they speak. A sound is not a sound without somebody to lend an ear to it: rhetoric is nothing without an audience.

There are a certain number of factors that affect the receiver's ear. These can be cultural factors such as the transition between different acting styles or the level of training that our contemporary ear has had. There are also personal and emotional factors. Often we feel the performance was not well-spoken because, somehow, it did not live up to our expectations of how we think it should have been performed. Is it that many of us have a self-conscious model, perhaps our own first experience of Shakespeare, that meant something to us and became our reference point for the future (some treasured performance kept under glass)? Nothing from then on can quite compare with that experience.

Most of the time, however, it is more complex than nostalgia. Take, for example, the thorny area of accent. I remind myself constantly that audibility is not embedded in Received Pronunciation or Standard American. The familiarity that those in power have with speech and the articulate confidence gained from coming from the right quarters can lead us all to hear certain types of voices as outshining others. But, to my mind, the role of theater is at least to question these assumptions so that we do not perpetuate those givens but work towards a broader tolerance.

In Canada on a production of *Twelfth Night*, I was working with an actor who was from Newfoundland. His own natural rhythms in speaking seemed completely at home with Shakespeare's. Is this because his root voice has direct links back to the voice of Shakespeare's time? It does seem that compared to British dialects, which are predominantly about pitch, many North American dialects have a wonderful respect and vibrancy in their use of vowels. Shakespeare's language seems to me very vowel-aware. How useful it is for an actor to isolate the vowels in the spoken words to hear the music they produce, the rich patterns, their direct connection to feelings. North Americans more easily respond to this and allow it to feed their speaking. I can only assume it is closer to how the Elizabethans spoke.

In *Othello* the very names of the characters have a direct connection to one vowel in particular. All the male names, except the Duke, end in the sound OH: Othello, Cassio, Iago, Brabantio, etc. Furthermore, the sound OH ripples through the play both consciously and unconsciously. "Oh" occurs repeatedly and, more interestingly, is contained within other words: "so," "soul," and "know." These words resonate throughout the play, reinforcing another level of meaning. The repeating of the same sounds affects us beyond what we can quite say.

Vowels come from deep within us, from our very core. We speak vowels before we speak consonants. They seem to reveal the feelings that require the consonants to give the shape to what we perceive as making sense.

Working with actors who are bilingual (or ones for whom English is not the native language) is fascinating because of the way it allows the actor to have an awareness of the cadence in Shakespeare. There seems to be an objective perception to the musical patterns in the text, and the use of alliteration and assonance are often more easily heard not just as literary devices, but also as means by which meaning is formed and revealed to an audience.

Every speech pattern (i.e., accent, rhythm) is capable of audibility. Each has its own music, each can become an accent when juxtaposed against another. The point at which a speech pattern becomes audible is in the dynamic of the physical making of those sounds. The speaker must have the desire to get through to a listener and must be confident that every speech pattern has a right to be heard.

SPEAKING SHAKESPEARE

So, the way to speak Shakespeare is not intrinsically tied to a particular sound; rather, it is how a speaker energetically connects to that language. Central to this is how we relate to the form of Shakespeare. Shakespeare employs verse, prose, and rhetorical devices to communicate meaning. For example, in *Romeo and Juliet,* the use of contrasts helps us to quantify Juliet's feelings: "And learn me how to lose a winning match," "Whiter than new snow upon a raven's back." These extreme opposites, "lose" and "winning," "new snow" and "raven's back," are her means to express and make sense of her feelings.

On a more personal note, I am often reminded how much, as an individual, I owe to Shakespeare's spoken word. The rather quiet and inarticulate schoolboy I once was, found in the speaking and the acting of those words a means to quench his thirst for expression.

NOTES:

(1) Peter Brook, "The Empty Space" (Harmondsworth: Penguin, 1972)
(2) Ted Hughes, "Winter Pollen" (London: Faber and Faber, 1995)
(3) Michael Redgrave, "The Actor's Ways and Means"
    (London: Heinemann, 1951)

In the Age of Shakespeare

Thomas Garvey

One of the earliest published pictures of Shakespeare's birthplace, from an original watercolor by Phoebe Dighton (1834)

The works of William Shakespeare have won the love of millions since he first set pen to paper some four hundred years ago; but at first blush, his plays can seem difficult to understand, even willfully obscure. There are so many strange words, not fancy, exactly, but often only half-familiar. And the very fabric of the language seems to spring from a world of forgotten assumptions, a vast network of beliefs and superstitions that have long been dispelled from the modern mind.

In fact, when "Gulielmus filius Johannes Shakespeare" (Latin for "William, son of John Shakespeare") was baptized in Stratford-on-Avon in 1564, English itself was only just settling into its current form; no dictionary had yet been written, and Shakespeare coined hundreds of words himself. Astronomy and medicine were entangled with astrology and the occult arts; democracy was waiting to be reborn; and even educated people believed in witches and fairies, and that the sun revolved around the Earth. Yet somehow Shakespeare still speaks to us today, in a voice as fresh and direct as the day his lines were first spoken; and to better understand both their artistic depth and enduring power, we must first understand something of his age.

REVOLUTION AND RELIGION

Shakespeare was born into a nation on the verge of global power, yet torn by religious strife. Henry VIII, the much-married father of Elizabeth I, had

From *The Book of Martyrs* (1563), this woodcut shows the Archbishop of Canterbury being burned at the stake in March 1556

Map of London ca. 1625

defied the Pope by proclaiming a new national church, with himself as its
head. After Henry's death, however, his daughter Mary reinstituted
Catholicism via a murderous nation-wide campaign, going so far as to burn
the Archbishop of Canterbury at the stake. But after a mere five years, the
childless Mary also died; and when her half-sister Elizabeth was crowned,
she declared the Church of England again triumphant.

In the wake of so many religious reversals, it is impossible to know
which form of faith lay closest to the English heart, and at first, Elizabeth
was content with mere outward deference to the Anglican Church. Once
the Pope hinted her assassination would not be a mortal sin, however, the
suppression of Catholicism grew more savage, and many Catholics—
including some known in Stratford—were hunted down and executed,
which meant being hanged, disemboweled, and carved into quarters. Many
scholars suspect that Shakespeare himself was raised a Catholic (his
father's testament of faith was found hidden in his childhood home). We
can speculate about the impact this religious tumult may have had on his

plays. Indeed, while explicit Catholic themes, such as the description of Purgatory in *Hamlet*, are rare, the larger themes of disguise and double allegiance are prominent across the canon. Prince Hal offers false friendship to Falstaff in the histories, the heroines of the comedies are forced to disguise themselves as men, and the action of the tragedies is driven by double-dealing villains. "I am not what I am," Iago tells us (and himself) in *Othello*, summing up in a single stroke what may have been Shakespeare's formative social and spiritual experience.

If religious conflict rippled beneath the body politic like some ominous undertow, on its surface the tide of English power was clearly on the rise. The defeat of the Spanish Armada in 1588 had established Britain as a global power; by 1595 Sir Walter Raleigh had founded the colony of Virginia (named for the Virgin Queen), and discovered a new crop, tobacco, which would inspire a burgeoning international trade. After decades of strife and the threat of invasion, England enjoyed a welcome stability. As the national coffers grew, so did London; over the course of Elizabeth's reign, the city would nearly double in size to a population of some 200,000.

Hornbook from Shakespeare's lifetime

A 1639 engraving of a scene from a royal state visit of Marie de Medici depicts London's packed, closely crowded half-timbered houses.

FROM COUNTRY TO COURT

The urban boom brought a new dimension to British life—the mentality of the metropolis. By contrast, in Stratford-on-Avon, the rhythms of the rural world still held sway. Educated in the local grammar school, Shakespeare was taught to read and write by a schoolmaster called an "abecedarian", and as he grew older, he was introduced to logic, rhetoric, and Latin. Like most schoolboys of his time, he was familiar with Roman mythology and may have learned a little Greek, perhaps by translating passages of the New Testament. Thus while he never attended a university, Shakespeare could confidently refer in his plays to myths and legends that today we associate with the highly educated.

Beyond the classroom, however, he was immersed in the life of the countryside, and his writing all but revels in its flora and fauna, from the wounded deer of *As You Like It* to the herbs and flowers which Ophelia scatters in *Hamlet*. Pagan rituals abounded in the rural villages of Shakespeare's day, where residents danced around maypoles in spring, performed "mummers' plays" in winter, and recited rhymes year-round to ward off witches and fairies.

The custom most pertinent to Shakespeare's art was the medieval "mystery play," in which moral allegories were enacted in country homes and village squares by troupes of traveling actors. These strolling players—usually four men and two boys who played the women's roles—often lightened the moralizing with bawdy interludes in a mix of high and low feeling, which would become a defining feature of Shakespeare's art. Occasionally even a professional troupe, such as Lord Strange's Men, or the Queen's Men, would arrive in town, perhaps coming straight to Shakespeare's door (his father was the town's bailiff) for permission to perform.

Rarely, however, did such troupes stray far from their base in London, the nation's rapidly expanding capital and cultural center. The city itself had existed since the time of the Romans (who built the original London Bridge), but it was not until the Renaissance that its population spilled beyond its ancient walls and began to grow along (and across) the Thames, by whose banks the Tudors had built their glorious palaces. It was these two contradictory worlds—a modern metropolis cheek-by-jowl with a medieval court—that provided the two very different audiences who applauded Shakespeare's plays.

Londoners both high and low craved distraction. Elizabeth's court constantly celebrated her reign with dazzling pageants and performances that required a local pool of professional actors and musicians. Beyond the graceful landscape of the royal parks, however, the general populace was packed into little more than a square mile of cramped and crooked streets where theatrical entertainment was frowned upon as compromising public morals.

Just outside the jurisdiction of the city fathers, however, across the twenty arches of London Bridge on the south bank of the Thames, lay the wilder district of "Southwark." A grim reminder of royal power lay at the end of the bridge—the decapitated heads of traitors stared down from pikes at passersby. Once beyond their baleful gaze, people found the amusements they desired, and their growing numbers meant a market suddenly existed for daily entertainment. Bear-baiting and cockfighting flourished, along with taverns, brothels, and even the new institution of the theater.

Southwark, as depicted in Hollar's long view of London (1647). Blackfriars is on the top right and the labels of Bear-Baiting and The Globe were inadvertently reversed.

The Advent of the Theatre

The first building in England designed for the performance of plays—called, straightforwardly enough, "The Theatre"—was built in London when Shakespeare was still a boy. It was owned by James Burbage, father of Richard Burbage, who would become Shakespeare's lead actor in the acting company The Lord Chamberlain's Men. "The Theatre," consciously or unconsciously, resembled the yards in which traveling players had long plied their trade—it was an open-air polygon, with three tiers of galleries surrounding a canopied stage in a flat central yard, which was ideal for the athletic competitions the building also hosted. The innovative arena must have found an appreciative audience, for it was soon joined by the Curtain, and then the Rose, which was the first theater to rise in Southwark among the brothels, bars, and bear-baiting pits.

Even as these new venues were being built, a revolution in the drama itself was taking place. Just as Renaissance artists turned to classical models for inspiration, so English writers looked to Roman verse as a prototype for the new national drama. "Blank verse," or iambic pentameter (that is, a poetic line with five alternating stressed and unstressed syllables), was an adaptation of Latin forms, and first appeared in England in a translation of Virgil's *Aeneid*. Blank verse was first spoken on stage in 1561, in the now-forgotten *Gorboduc*, but it was not until the brilliant Christopher Marlowe (born the same year as Shakespeare) transformed it into the "mighty line" of such plays as *Tamburlaine* (1587) that the power and flexibility of the form made it the baseline of English drama.

Marlowe—who, unlike Shakespeare, had attended college—led the "university wits," a clique of hard-living free thinkers who in between all manner of exploits managed to define a new form of theater. The dates of Shakespeare's arrival in London are unknown—we have no record of him in Stratford after 1585—but by the early 1590s he had already absorbed the essence of Marlowe's invention, and begun producing astonishing innovations of his own.

While the "university wits" had worked with myth and fantasy, however, Shakespeare turned to a grand new theme, English history—penning the three-part saga of *Henry VI* in or around 1590. The trilogy was such a success that Shakespeare became the envy of his circle—one unhappy competitor, Robert Greene, even complained in 1592 of "an upstart crow…beautified with our feathers…[who is] in his own conceit the only Shake-scene in a country."

Such jibes perhaps only confirmed Shakespeare's estimation of himself, for he began to apply his mastery of blank verse in all directions, succeeding at tragedy (*Titus Andronicus*), farce (*The Comedy of Errors*), and romantic comedy (*The Two Gentlemen of Verona*). He drew his plots from everywhere: existing poems, romances, folk tales, even other plays. In fact a number of Shakespeare's dramas (*Hamlet* included) may be revisions of earlier texts owned by his troupe. Since copyright laws did not exist, acting companies usually kept their texts close to their chests, only allowing publication when a play was no longer popular, or, conversely, when a play was *so* popular (as with *Romeo and Juliet*) that unauthorized versions had already been printed.

Demand for new plays and performance venues steadily increased. Soon, new theaters (the Hope and the Swan) joined the Rose in Southwark, followed shortly by the legendary Globe, which opened in 1600. (After some trouble with their lease, Shakespeare's acting troupe, the Lord Chamberlain's Men, had disassembled "The Theatre" and transported its pendeſt on ſo meane a ſtay. Baſe minded men all three of you, if by my miſerie you be not warnd: for vnto none of you (like mee) ſought thoſe burres to cleaue : thoſe Puppets (I meane) that ſpake from our mouths, thoſe Anticks garniſht in our colours. Is it not ſtrange, that I, to whom they all haue beene beholding: is it not like that you, to whome they all haue beene beholding, ſhall (were yee in that caſe as I am now) bee both at once of them forſaken: Yes truſt them not: for there is an vp-ſtart Crow, beautified with our feathers, that with his Tygers hart wrapt in a Players hyde, ſuppoſes he is as well able to bombaſt out a blanke verſe as the beſt of you: and beeing an abſolute Iohannes fac totum, is in his owne conceit the onely Shake-ſcene in a countrey. O that I might intreat your rare wits to be imploied in more profitable courſes : & let thoſe Apes imitate your paſt excellence, and neuer more acquaint them with your admired inuentions. I knowe the beſt husband of

Greene's insult, lines 9–14

timbers across the Thames, using them as the structure for the Globe.) Shakespeare was a shareholder in this new venture, with its motto "All the world's a stage" and continued to write and perform for it as well. Full-length plays were now being presented every afternoon but Sunday, and the public appetite for new material seemed endless.

The only curb on the public's hunger for theater was its fear of the plague—for popular belief held the disease was easily spread in crowds. Even worse, the infection was completely beyond the powers of Elizabethan medicine, which held that health derived from four "humors" or internal fluids identified as bile, phlegm, blood, and choler. Such articles of faith, however, were utterly ineffective against a genuine health crisis, and in times of plague, the authorities' panicked response was to shut down any venue where large crowds might congregate. The theaters would be closed for lengthy periods in 1593, 1597, and 1603, during which times Shakespeare was forced to play at court, tour the provinces, or, as many scholars believe, write what would become his famous cycle of sonnets.

The Next Stage

Between these catastrophic closings, the theater thrived as the great medium of its day; it functioned as film, television, and radio combined as well as a venue for music and dance (all performances, even tragedies, ended with a dance). Moreover, the theater was the place to see and be seen; for a penny you could

Famous scale model of The Globe completed by Dr. John Cranford Adams in 1954. Collectively, 25,000 pieces were used in constructing the replica. Dr. Adams used walnut to imitate the timber of the Globe, plaster was placed with a spoon and medicine dropper, and 6,500 "tiny" bricks measured by pencil eraser strips were individually placed on the model.

stand through a performance in the yard, a penny more bought you a seat in the galleries, while yet another purchased you a cushion. The wealthy, the poor, the royal, and the common all gathered at the Globe, and Shakespeare designed his plays—with their action, humor, and highly refined poetry—not only to satisfy their divergent tastes but also to respond to their differing points of view. In the crucible of Elizabethan theater, the various classes could briefly see themselves as others saw them, and drama could genuinely show "the age and body of the time his form and pressure," to quote Hamlet himself.

In order to accommodate his expanding art, the simplicity of the Elizabethan stage had developed a startling flexibility. The canopied platform of the Globe had a trap in its floor for sudden disappearances, while an alcove at the rear, between the pillars supporting its roof, allowed for "discoveries" and interior space. Above, a balcony made possible the love scene in *Romeo and Juliet*; while still higher, the thatched roof could double as a tower or rampart. And though the stage was largely free of scenery, the costumes were sumptuous—a theater troupe's clothing was its greatest asset. Patrons were used to drums in battle scenes, and real cannons firing overhead (in fact, a misfire would one day set the Globe aflame).

With the death of Elizabeth, and the accession of James I to the throne in 1603, Shakespeare only saw his power and influence grow. James, who considered himself an intellectual and something of a scholar, took over the patronage of the Lord Chamberlain's Men, renaming them the King's Men; the troupe even marched in his celebratory entrance to London. At this pinnacle of both artistic power and prestige, Shakespeare composed *Othello*, *King Lear*, and *Macbeth* in quick succession, and soon the King's Men acquired a new, indoor theater in London, which allowed the integration of more music and spectacle into his work. At this wildly popular venue, Shakespeare developed a new form of drama that scholars have dubbed "the romance," which combined elements of comedy and tragedy in a magnificent vision that would culminate in the playwright's last masterpiece, *The Tempest*. Not long after this final innovation, Shakespeare retired to Stratford a wealthy and prominent gentleman.

BEYOND THE ELIZABETHAN UNIVERSE

This is how Shakespeare fit into his age. But how did he transcend it? The answer lies in the plays themselves. For even as we see in the surface of his drama the belief system of England in the sixteenth century, Shakespeare himself is always questioning his own culture, holding its ideas up to the light and shaking them, sometimes hard. In the case of the Elizabethan faith in astrology, Shakespeare had his villain Edmund sneer, "We make guilty of our disasters the sun, the moon, and stars; as if we were villains on necessity." When pondering the medieval code of chivalry, Falstaff decides, "The better part of valor is discretion." The divine right of kings is questioned in *Richard II*, and the inferior status of women—a belief that survived even the crowning of Elizabeth—appears ridiculous before the brilliant examples of Portia (*The Merchant of Venice*), and Rosalind (*As You Like It*). Perhaps it is through this constant shifting of perspective, this relentless sense of exploration, that the playwright somehow outlived the limits of his own period, and became, in the words of his rival Ben Jonson, "not just for an age, but for all time."

Acknowledgments

The series editors wish to give heartfelt thanks to the advisory editors on *Romeo and Juliet*, David Bevington, Barbara Gaines, and Peter Holland, whose brilliance, keen judgment, and timely advice were irreplaceable during the process of assembling this book.

We are incredibly grateful to the community of Shakespeare scholars for their generosity in sharing their talents, collections, and even their address books. We would not have been able to pull together such an august list of contributors without their help. Thank you to David Bevington, Tom Garvey, Doug Lanier, Jill Levenson, and Andrew Wade for their marvelous essays. Extra appreciation goes to Doug Lanier for all his guidance and the use of his personal Shakespeare collection. Thank you to the following professors for answering questions and discussing our ideas, no matter how unusual they may have sounded: Michael Best, Regina Buccola, Mark Burnett, Paul Cantor, Michael Cordner, Larry Friedlander, Suzanne Gosset, Katherine Maus, and David Nicol. We want to acknowledge the editors of our future editions who have already contributed much to the series: Terri Bourus, Rob Ormsby, and William Williams. We are especially grateful to William for his astute guidance and hand-holding on all issues textual.

We want to single out Tanya Gough, the proprietor of The Poor Yorick Shakespeare Catalog, for all her efforts on behalf of the series. She was an early supporter, providing encouragement from the very beginning, and jumping in with whatever we needed. For her encyclopedic knowledge of Shakespeare on film and audio, for sharing her experience and collaborating on the explanatory notes, for introducing us into her estimable network, and for a myriad of other contributions too numerous to mention, we offer our deepest gratitude.

Our research was aided immensely by the wonderful staff at Shakespeare archives and libraries around the world: Jane Edmonds and Ellen Charendoff from the Stratford Festival Archives; David Way, Richard Fairman, and the Sound Archives group from the British Library; Susan Brock and the staff at The Shakespeare Birthplace Trust; Georgianna Ziegler, Richard Kuhta, Jeremy Erlich, and everyone at the Folger Shakespeare Library; Lynne Farrington from the Annenberg Rare Book & Manuscript Library at the University of Pennsylvania; and Gene Rinkel,

Bruce Swann, Nuala Koetter, and Madeline Gibson, from the Rare Book and Special Collections Library at the University of Illinois. These individuals were instrumental in helping us gather audio: Justyn Baker, Janet Benson, Annie Hughes, Linn Lancett-Miles, Tamar Thomas, and Carly Wilford. We appreciate all your help.

From the world of drama, the following shared their passion with us and helped us develop the series into a true partnership between between the artistic and academic communities. We are indebted to: Graham Abbey, Kate Buckley, Steve Pickering, Joseph Plummer, Bob Scogin, Scott Wentworth, Marilyn Halperin and the team at Chicago Shakespeare Theater, Beth Emelson from The Folger Theatre, Beth Burns and the team at the Guthrie Theater, Michael Kahn, Catherine Weidner, Lauren Beyea, and the team at The Shakespeare Theatre, Steven Tabakin and The Public Theater, Jeffrey Horowitz from Theater for a New Audience, George Joseph, the 2005 *Romeo and Juliet* cast from Chicago Shakespeare, and Lucien Riviere from the RSC. Special thanks go to Nancy Becker of The Shakespeare Society.

With respect to the audio, we extend our heartfelt thanks to our narrating team: our director, John Tydeman, our esteemed narrator, Sir Derek Jacobi, and Daryl Chapman and RNIB Talking Book Studios. John has been a wonderful, generous resource to us and we look forward to future collaborations. We owe a debt of gratitude to Nicolas Soames for introducing us and for being unfailingly helpful. Thanks also to the "Speaking Shakespeare" team: Andrew Wade, the Guthrie Experience, and the Guthrie Theater for producing that wonderful recording as the clock wound down.

Our personal thanks for their kindness and unstinting support go to: Charlie Athanas, Ray Bennett, Marie Bennett, Marissa Colgate, Josie Macaisa, Maribeth Macaisa, Sheila Madigan, Mary Ellen Zurko, and our families.

Finally, thanks to everyone at Sourcebooks who contributed their talents in realizing The Sourcebooks Shakespeare—in particular, Samantha Raue, Todd Stocke, Andrea Edl, Dan Williams, and Megan Dempster.

Audio Credits

In all cases, we have attempted to provide archival audio in its original form. While we have tried to achieve the best possible quality on the archival audio, some audio quality is the result of source limitations. Archival audio research by Marie Macaisa. Narration script by Marie Macaisa and Joseph Plummer. Audio editing by Marie Macaisa and RNIB. Narration recording, Audio engineering, and mastering by RNIB Talking Book Studios in London, UK. Recording for "Speaking Shakespeare" by Guthrie Theater.

The following are under license from Naxos of America www.naxosusa.com Ⓟ HNH International Ltd. All rights reserved.
Tracks 1, 3, 5, 6, 11, 16, 20

The following are under license from HarperAudio / Caedmon. All rights reserved.
Tracks 8, 10, 17

The following are selections from The Complete Arkangel Shakespeare Ⓟ 2003, with permission of The Audio Partners Publishing Corporation. All rights reserved. Unabridged audio dramatizations of all 38 plays. For more information, visit www.audiopartners.com/shakespeare
Tracks 7, 9

The following are selections from BBC Radio Presents Romeo & Juliet, presented by the Renaissance Theatre Company. Permission kindly granted by Kenneth Branagh. Under license from BBC Worldwide Ltd. All rights reserved.
Tracks 13, 14, 15

The following is under license from IPC Media. All rights reserved.
Tracks 2, 4, 9

The following is under license from BBC Worldwide Ltd. All rights reserved.
Track 18

"Speaking Shakespeare" (Track 21) courtesy of Andrew Wade and the Guthrie Experience for Actors in Training.

Photo Credits

Every effort has been made to correctly attribute all the materials reproduced in this book. If any errors have been made, we will be happy to correct them in future editions.

Images from the following pages courtesy of Horace Howard Furness Memorial Library, University of Pennsylvania: 2–5, 13–16, 34, 40, 46, 50, 64, 110, 130, 154, 184, 186, 268, 278, 300–304

Images on the following pages courtesy of The Folger Shakespeare Library: 216, 351–355, 357, 361

Photos from the October 17, 1935 staging at the New Theatre directed by Sir John Gielgud are courtesy of Rare Book and Special Collections Library, University of Illinois at Urbana-Champaign. Photos are credited on the pages in which they appear.

Photos from Chicago Shakespeare Theater productions are courtesy of Chicago Shakespeare Theater. Photos are credited on the pages in which they appear.

Photos from Guthrie Theater productions are courtesy of the Guthrie Theater. Photos are credited on the pages in which they appear.

Photos from the Castellani, Cukor, and Zeffirelli productions are courtesy of Douglas Lanier. Photos are credited on the pages in which they appear.

Photos from The Shakespeare Theatre productions in Washington, DC, are courtesy of The Shakespeare Theatre. Photos are credited on the pages in which they appear.

Photos from The Royal Shakespeare Company productions are © 2005 Shakespeare Birthplace Trust. Photos are credited on the pages in which they appear.

About The Contributors

ESSAYISTS

Thomas Garvey (In the Age of Shakespeare) has been acting, directing, or writing about Shakespeare for over two decades. A graduate of the Massachusetts Institute of Technology, he studied acting and directing with the MIT Shakespeare Ensemble, where he played Hamlet, Jacques, Iago, and other roles, and directed *All's Well That Ends Well* and *Twelfth Night*. He has since directed and designed several other Shakespearean productions, as well as works by Chekhov, Ibsen, Sophocles, Beckett, Moliere, and Shaw. Mr. Garvey currently writes on theatre for the Boston Globe and other publications.

Douglas Lanier (*Romeo and Juliet* and Pop Culture) is an Associate Professor of English at the University of New Hampshire. He has written many essays on Shakespeare in popular culture, including "Shakescorp Noir" in Shakespeare Quarterly and "Shakespeare on the Record" in *The Blackwell Companion to Shakespeare in Performance*. His book, *Shakespeare and Modern Popular Culture*, was published in 2002. He's currently working on a book-length study of cultural stratification in early modern British theater.

Jill L. Levenson (In Production) is a Professor of English at Trinity College at the University of Toronto. She has written and edited numerous essays and books including *Romeo and Juliet* for the Manchester University Press's series *Shakespeare in Performance*, *Shakespeare and the Twentieth Century* (with Jonathan Bate and Dieter Mehl), and the Oxford edition of *Romeo and Juliet* . Currently she is writing a book on Shakespeare and modern drama for Shakespeare Topics, a series published by Oxford University Press.

Andrew Wade (A Voice Coach's Perspective) was Head of Voice for the Royal Shakespeare Company, 1990–2003 and Voice Assistant Director from 1987–1990. During this time he worked on 170 productions and with more than 80 directors. Along with Cicely Berry, Andrew recorded *Working Shakespeare*, the DVD series *Voice and Shakespeare*, and he was the verse consultant for the movie *Shakespeare In Love*. In 2000, he won a Bronze Award from the New York International Radio Festival for the series *Lifespan*, which he co-directed and devised. He works widely teaching, lecturing, and coaching throughout the world.